900

XP
16.95

D69

# JAMES JOYCE'S SCHOOLDAYS

# BRUCE BRADLEY S.J.

# JAMES JOYCE'S SCHOOLDAYS

## Foreword by Richard Ellmann

ST. MARTIN'S PRESS          NEW YORK

Printed in Great Britain
First published in the United States of America in 1982

ISBN 0–312–43978–4

**Library of Congress Cataloging in Publication Data**

Bradley, Bruce
    James Joyce's Schooldays

    Bibliography: p.
    1. Joyce, James, 1882–1941—Biography—Youth
2. Novelists, Irish—20th century—Biography—Youth
I. Title
PR6019.09Z52619    1982            823'.912        81–23341
                                                    AACR2

*For my mother,*
*Vida Elizabeth Bradley*

# Contents

The author and publishers are grateful for permission to quote extracts from *A Portrait of the Artist as a Young Man*, by James Joyce, the definitive text, corrected from the Dublin holograph by Chester G. Anderson and edited by Richard Ellmann. Copyright 1916 by B. W. Huebsch, copyright renewed 1944 by Nora Joyce. Copyright © 1964 by the Estate of James Joyce. Reprinted by kind permission of Viking Penguin Inc. and the Executors of the James Joyce Estate.

# A Note on References

Parenthetical references in the text are to Joyce's writings throughout. A simple numerical reference, such as (265), indicates that the source is *A Portrait*; in references to *Ulysses* and *Stephen Hero*, the page number is preceded by *U* and *S* respectively, except where the context is so obvious as to make this superfluous.

The references to *A Portrait* and *Dubliners* are taken from Harry Levin, ed., *The Portable James Joyce*, Harmondsworth: Penguin Books Ltd. 1976; references to *Ulysses* are taken from the Bodley Head edition, London 1976; references to *Stephen Hero* are taken from the Panther/Granada edition, St Albans 1977.

# Acknowledgments

Although this is a small book, I am indebted to many people for help in completing it. I wish to thank Frs Joseph Dargan (now the Irish Jesuit provincial) and Paddy Carberry, successively rectors of Clongowes while I was at work; Fr Philip Fogarty, the headmaster, and Fr Ronnie Burke Savage, the archivist, for giving me full access to material in Clongowes; Fr Paul Andrews, the rector of my own community in Belvedere, for help in tracing sources there and for his interest and support; and Fr Fergal McGrath, archivist of the Irish Province of the Society of Jesus. For the loan of books or for helpful suggestions and advice, I thank Dr John Garvin, Fr Michael Paul Gallagher, Stewart Donovan, Fr Bob Thompson, Kate and David Bateman, and Fr Percy Winder. Bill Doyle did almost all the work on the photographs, restoring old pictures and making the new ones on pp. 64, 72 and 76. Sean O'Mordha of RTE took a kindly interest in the book's progress, provided the picture on p. 57 and restored the one on p. 18. Col. Jack Burke-Gaffney kindly gave me an excellent print of the Belvedere *Vice Versa* cast. It was at all times a pleasure to work with Michael Gill and Fergal Tobin of Gill and Macmillan.

Finally, a special word of thanks to two people. My friend Fr Paddy Crowe helped my initial researches when he was headmaster of Clongowes and has greatly supported me and the enterprise ever since. It is difficult to express adequately my gratitude to Professor Richard Ellmann for his interest and encouragement, many detailed suggestions and, above all, his kindness in writing a foreword to the book.

# Foreword

James Joyce's formal education began at Clongowes Wood College in 1888 when he was six and a half. He remained there until 1891. Then, after an interval, he entered Belvedere College in 1893 and stayed until 1898, after which he entered University College, Dublin. All three institutions were run by the Jesuit order. When two Dominican priests urged Joyce to transfer from Belvedere to their school, he declared, 'I began with the Jesuits and I want to end with them.'

His respect for his schooling remained even after he became an unbeliever. He said of the Jesuits, 'They taught me how to order and to judge', and later, when amazed by his own ability to persevere in his writing in adverse circumstances, he thought it might be due to the 'influence of *ad maiorem dei gloriam*' (the Jesuit motto). From these teachers he learned not only the academic curriculum, but also the ritual and moral codes which, in all his rebellion, he would never cease to find fascinating.

For Joyce's books could not exist without Catholicism as panoply or as theme. The fabric of life as presented in *Dubliners* is shot through with religion; Stephen Dedalus's rebellion as an artist involves setting up a counter-church of art, with analogues in every part of the church he was renouncing. Bloom's mind ranges over confession and communion, Stephen's over old heresies, church history, his mother's piety. In *Finnegans Wake* old battles, as of homoousian and homoiousian, or St Patrick and the Druid, are fought once more in an atmosphere of jollity which they originally lacked. Mulligan claims that Stephen has the Jesuit strain in him, 'only it's injected the wrong way'. The jibe seems applicable to Joyce as well.

The years during which the detail and spirit of his religion were inculcated in Joyce have, therefore, a special interest. No one knows more about the formal side of this education than Fr Bruce Bradley, S.J. He knows at first hand the care and skill which continue to be lavished on boys' education at Clongowes and Belvedere, and has an eye also on the ways in which pupils circumvent their masters. His search in the schools' archives has enabled him to make a number of discoveries, small but important.

The most exciting is the *Punishment Book* at Clongowes. Although some pages of it are missing, enough remain to list three pandyings of young Joyce. He was given four strokes on 14 March 1889, just after his seventh birthday, for the rarely mentioned offence of 'vulgar language.' (He would commit it ever more abundantly during the rest of his life.) The other two infractions were of less moment. There is no mention of the famous pandying for having his glasses broken by another boy which occupies so great a place in *A Portrait of the Artist as a Young Man*. Joyce told Herbert Gorman that this had indeed happened to him at Clongowes, but it seems to have been left out or cut out from the *Punishment Book*. By omitting his three other pandyings, especially the one for 'vulgar language', Joyce greatly ennobles the small Dedalus boy, and makes clear that his novel is, as it should be, stylised rather than transcriptive. Bruce Bradley has also discovered that the man on whom the ferocious Father Dolan was presumably modelled was much younger than Joyce described him. Joyce's motive in ageing him may have been to contrast him with the benevolent old priest to whom Stephen confesses after the retreat at Belvedere.

Of course Joyce lived his schooldays to a great extent outside the school precincts, and in ways unsuspected by his masters at Clongowes and Belvedere. He was gathering himself for a life and a way of thinking that they could not have imagined. Bruce Bradley is aware of the volcanic properties of this child and adolescent, but he recognises also that good schooling had its effect, as much as truancy, upon what was to happen later. Other writers have dealt with Belvedere and Clongowes, notably Kevin Sullivan. But Bruce Bradley has the advantage of belonging to the school system he is writing about. As a master at Belvedere, he can compare past and present with intimacy and expertise.

The account which he offers is unassuming, painstaking, accurate, and well written. It gives the precise flavour of Jesuit education in the years that Joyce was a pupil as no large generalisations could do. He is not out to prove anything, but to illuminate. Lovers of Joyce's writings – that always growing multitude in which people of all religions, and of none, joyfully participate – will find it congenial to study the beginnings of Joyce in Bruce Bradley's good company.

RICHARD ELLMANN
*New College*
*Oxford*

# Introduction

James Joyce has been rather neglected by the Irish Jesuits, his school-masters for almost ten years. In 1904, when he was beginning work on his first novel, his brother Stanislaus wrote in his diary for 2 February: 'He is putting a large number of acquaintances into it, and those Jesuits whom he has known. I don't think they will like themselves in it'.[1] As regards the Jesuits at least, Stanislaus seems to have been right. Ever since Joyce left their care and proceeded to immortalise the educational establishments in which they had trained him, the Jesuits in Ireland have maintained an almost complete silence on the subject of their most famous pupil.

Joyce was in Clongowes Wood College from 1888 to 1891. Four years after he left, a college magazine, *The Clongownian*, was begun. The issue for Christmas 1899, in its column 'Clongownians at the University', reported that in the Matriculation examination he had obtained second-class honours in Latin.[2] 'And that', as Joyce's first biographer Herbert Gorman (possibly echoing the embittered sentiments of Joyce himself) wrote, 'was the first and last mention of the former Clongownian in the school magazine. So far as Clongowes Wood College was concerned, James Joyce passed out with the nineteenth century'.[3]

Gorman was writing in 1941 and what he said was true. Not until 1955 would Joyce be heard of again in the magazine's columns, thus bridging a fifty-six year gap. From time to time an item rather grandly entitled 'Clongownians in literature' appeared. In 1920 a 'Catalogue of the works of past Clongownians' was published.[4] The following year Master John Thornton Towers was awarded the Clongowes Past Pupils' Union Gold Medal for his essay on 'Clongowes and its neighbourhood in poetry and fiction'.[5] In none of these was there any mention of Joyce. In 1930 Arthur Clery, one of Joyce's associates in the Literary and Historical Society, wrote about 'Clongownians at old U.C.D.' Again there was no mention of Joyce, although this time it was possible to recognise a hidden reference in Clery's observation that 'none of us then expected that our college would become quite so famous as the writings of its past students have made it'.[6] Joyce's death in 1941 went unrecorded. In 1955 the editor of *The Clongownian* invited a near contemporary of Joyce to write his reminiscences of the college in the 1890s. The article included a few lines in which the writer recalled what he had heard of Joyce in Clongowes.[7] It was the first time any reference had been made to him in the magazine for over half a century.

*The Belvederian*, like *The Clongownian*, began just a few years too late to record Joyce's actual schooldays. Like *The Clongownian*, references to Joyce in its pages are few and far between, although *The Belvederian* comes slightly better out of the comparison. The second issue contained 'Verses by a Past Belvederian' – these were in fact the opening three stanzas of Joyce's *Chamber Music*, published the same year.[8] They presumably found their way into the annual through the good offices of his former teacher, George Dempsey.[9] In 1910 Joyce's name was included in a list of Mr Dempsey's Intermediate prize-winners.[10] Some years later William Dawson, another of Joyce's UCD contemporaries, wrote of his own time in the university and observed that 'men whose names have since become famous – Sheehy-Skeffington, Tom Kettle, Arthur Clery, Hugh Kennedy, to mention but a few – were undergrads in those days'. By then *A Portrait* and, more pertinently, *Ulysses*, had been published: there was no room to mention James Joyce.[11] His death, like the publication of his works, was passed over in silence. As in the case of *The Clongownian*, it was the mid-fifties before he was heard of again. In 1957 Fr J. C. Kelly, then a member of the Belvedere staff, broke with the unspoken tradition of several generations by contributing a long and appreciative review of Joyce's recently-published *Letters*.[12] The final columns of the article shared a page of *The Belvederian* with the annual list of deceased past pupils. By one of those coincidences which Joyce loved, the list on this occasion included two of his own contemporaries, already granted a somewhat dubious immortality by himself in *Ulysses*: Oliver St John Gogarty and Reuben Dodd. Two years later, Judge Eugene Sheehy's obituary notice said what William Dawson and Arthur Clery had felt unable to say in the twenties and thirties:

> Eugene Sheehy went from school to the Old Royal and here he entered into the fermenting intellectual atmosphere which produced a revolution and a literary revival. It was the Old Royal of Joyce made famous by him but it was the Royal where at this very time the oratory of Tom Kettle was first to be heard in the L. and H. Among this brilliant and versatile group Eugene Sheehy was at home, an equal among equals.[13]

The following year Joyce's photograph appeared in *The Belvederian*. An old picture of the gymnasts, dancers and cast of *Vice Versa*, who had contributed to the Whitsuntide entertainment in 1898, was published. As many individuals as possible (including James and Stanislaus Joyce, Albrecht Connolly and the two Sheehys) were identified. In addition, there was an enlargement of Joyce in his role as Dr Grimstone and explanatory reference to *A Portrait*.[14]

Neglect of Joyce in the magazines published by his old schools was not, at first, due to disapproval. It is always hard for the editors to keep in touch with past pupils once a few years have passed. 'We all lose sight of each other after we leave', as Wells said to Stephen (*S* 67). The difficulty would become acute when a past pupil disappeared into exile in remote Trieste. Few enough of Joyce's contemporaries in either school ever found their way into the 'news of the past' columns of *The Clongownian* or *The Belvederian* in later years. In Joyce's case the signs of genius were slow to emerge. He was certainly precocious, but it would be wrong to imagine that his academic record at school made him one of Belvedere's most distinguished students. His achievements were easily surpassed by others, such as his slightly older friend and contemporary Vincent Connolly. And, unlike Joyce, Connolly's subsequent academic performance was of a piece with his achievements in school.[15] By the time James Joyce finally found fame, time and distance had dimmed familiarity with him. And rumour made him notorious.

It is, of course, all too easy to smile indulgently at the susceptibilities of another age, granted the benefit of later knowledge. Joyce had set out to mock and outrage the susceptibilities of his own day. The Jesuits were bound to feel, at the very least, a keen sense of disappointment. It seemed that he had not merely turned his back on the values they held most sacred themselves and had tried to instil in him, but that he had first publicly trampled all over them. J. C. Kelly wrote in *The Belvederian*:

> Religion always haunted Joyce but he was one of those otherwise very intelligent men who still manage to be very unintelligent about religion. . . . He could not see the wheat for the tares. His was a Catholic mind that rejected superstition and thought it had rejected the Faith.[16]

The distinction made here between faith and superstition, like the distinction between authentic religion and the limiting, even distorting cultural forms in which it is apt to be clothed, is a subtle one. It can be used glibly. To appreciate the justice of Fr Kelly's remarks, the Jesuits would have had to make a more dispassionate inspection of the evidence than they could possibly have achieved at the time. And this supposes that they read their former pupil's books. His *succès de scandale* almost certainly deterred them even from that. They could not have known what Italo Svevo, the writer's friend in Trieste, knew, that 'Joyce still feels admiration and gratitude for the care of his educators; whilst his sinister Dedalus cannot find time to say so'.[17] The pity is that the early judgments, understandable at the time, took so long to revise. As a rector of Belvedere in the fifties told Patricia Hutchins, 'He has just been looked upon as one of the bad boys'.[18]

Joyce's schooldays have been dealt with before, summarily in the 'authorised' Gorman biography, more comprehensively in Kevin Sullivan's *Joyce Among the Jesuits* and Richard Ellmann's truly magisterial *James Joyce*. What is offered here attempts to fill in the record of his time in Clongowes and Belvedere in somewhat greater detail, on the basis of documents already known but not yet fully exploited and also of new material, recently discovered. But despite the documentary base, it must remain merely complementary to the work already done by Sullivan and, above all, by Ellmann. The present work is not, either, that 'study of Joyce, from a Jesuit, Catholic point of view . . . a serious estimate of the religious and psychological factors involved', once desiderated by Patricia Hutchins.[19] It is essentially a series of historical footnotes to *A Portrait*.

Ellmann thought that 'the records at Clongowes were not well kept' in Joyce's time,[20] while Scholes and Kain lamented the fact that 'of Joyce's stay at the preparatory school, Belvedere College, we have only meager records – two essays, some examination grades . . .'[21] They are both right. However, a number of documents have since turned up which throw light on his time at school, particularly in the case of Clongowes. Thus we have a Higher Line *Prefect's Journal* and a *Minister's Journal* which cover his period. In the latter he is obliquely mentioned on one occasion. We also have a *Punishment Book* in which his name occurs three times. There are the 'Rules of the Boys of Clongoweswood', which governed his life in the school. And there are some copies of *The Rhetorician,* a magazine produced by the senior boys in 1888 and maintained even after they left – these convey something of the atmosphere of the place as the boys knew it.[22] In addition, the *Students' Ledger* and the *Students' Register* repay more careful examination than Sullivan was able to give them when researching his own book.

For Belvedere the situation is less happy. Sullivan saw the *Prefect of Studies' Book* and the *Cash Book* which I make further use of here. He did not see the 'Science School' Ledger, which is of some interest. On the other hand, he did have access to the *Annals of the Congregation of the Blessed Virgin Mary,* which has been unfortunately mislaid in very recent years. Apart from these, the present study draws on the Intermediate papers Joyce sat while at Belvedere in the nineties. And, as in the case of Clongowes, I have perused the school magazine for any light it may throw on Joyce's schooldays.

4

Efforts to illustrate this period of Joyce's life photographically have tended in the past to be somewhat inaccurate. Thus, the corridor shown in Ellmann's biography purports to lead 'to the rector's office', scene of the famous protest against unjust punishment.[23] But the long gallery in the picture would have brought Joyce nowhere near Fr Conmee's room, which lay in the opposite direction and in another building. William York Tindall's photograph of the 'Castle and Chapel at Clongowes' in *The Joyce Country* has the 1907 Boys' Chapel, unthought of in James Joyce's time. The playing fields he shows are the modern Higher Line rugby pitches; Joyce played a different kind of football on what was then a gravel surface behind the Castle. And 'the square ditch' is not 'off among the trees' in Tindall's picture but in front of the Castle.[24] Chester Anderson has a photograph in *James Joyce and his world* with a caption referring to 'the dark entrance hall of the castle'. But the picture, which includes the 1929 building, shows the east front of the Castle instead of the west front, where the entrance hall actually is.[25] Finally the Clongowes episodes of Joseph Strick's 1977 film version of *A Portrait* were not made on location, except for a shot of the entrance gate. He also used the modern chapel in Belvedere for the retreat scene; this building did not exist in Joyce's day. These may seem rather trivial points. Yet they are hardly too trivial when it comes to illustrating the work of an author who was so scrupulous in points of detail himself. Thus, years after he had left school, Joyce wrote to his father 'to make sure the trees at Clongowes were beeches'.[26] It is impossible to avoid all anachronism, especially in the case of Belvedere, where contemporary pictures are hard to find. But the illustrations contained here are as accurate and as nearly contemporary with Joyce as possible.[27]

The present undertaking is not based on the false presupposition that *A Portrait* is Joyce's autobiography. One of the perennial issues in studies of this work has been the extent to which it is a historically accurate portrayal of Joyce's own experiences. No one would now make the mistake of confusing the character and personality of Stephen Dedalus with that of Joyce, though similarities naturally exist between the two. But it is generally agreed that the narrative is a highly stylised account of events which actually took place in Joyce's life. Both points need emphasis: the creative stylisation and the basis in fact. Events in Joyce's own life have been compressed, altered in texture or adjusted in sequence to suit the writer's intentions. Since the primary concern is with the artist's subjectivity, the external events by which this is modified have only a secondary importance.

In particular, the chronology of *A Portrait* is not to be confused with the chronology of Joyce's life. Joyce himself was three years and some months in Clongowes. Stephen seems to spend only one year there.

Joyce's presentation of this year is a masterpiece of compression. The whole Clongowes chapter is built around two incidents, each lasting approximately twenty-four hours.[28] In the winter term, Stephen is bullied by one of the bigger boys in his line. When we first encounter him, a half-hearted participant in gravel football, he is already feverish. The next day he is in bed, dreaming about Parnell. In the summer term, having broken his glasses by accident the day before, he is pandied unjustly by Fr Dolan (a more sophisticated form of bullying) and successfully protests to the rector. In the course of narrating these two incidents, Joyce manages to fill in the background of Stephen's life at school and conveys the sense of a whole year passing. His companions during this year include boys who were never in the school together. Similarly, Jesuits who were never colleagues in real life become members of the staff at the same time. Thus Wells and Jack Lawton were not contemporaries in Clongowes. Mr Barrett was never on the staff at the same time as Fr Arnall's real-life counterpart, Fr William Power. And Fr Power had left Clongowes before Tom Furlong arrived. But given Joyce's aim of conveying the 'artist's' early impressions of school, such anachronisms are irrelevant.[29]

At Belvedere Stephen's inner states become increasingly the centre of attention. He is no longer the impressionable child, steeped in his surroundings and as yet only dimly aware of himself. Self-awareness now will become gradually almost suffocating. Other people and external events are distant interruptions of the interior monologue. The chronology is vague. Seasons symbolise states of soul. Subjective time is what matters. It is difficult to know just how long Stephen spends in Belvedere. Joyce himself was over five years there but Stephen seems to move faster. He is already 'in number two', which means Middle Grade, 'at the end of his second year' (321). But this would mean that he had only twelve months left in the school. In fact, the events subsequently narrated seem to extend over a longer period. Joyce is not concerned to be precise.[30]

But the environment in which Stephen developed always remains quite concrete. Joyce describes Clongowes and Belvedere as he knew them with almost pedantic accuracy. The topography of Stephen's visit to the rector, for example, is scrupulously exact. His life in Clongowes is governed by the rules which actually operated in Joyce's time. The numbers by which the different classes were known in Belvedere are correctly recorded. Details of vocabulary may parody schoolboy language of the period; but they are also an echo of what Joyce himself heard at school.[31] The names of persons are sometimes changed either for reasons of symbolism or confidentiality and, no doubt, to avoid the possibility of libel. Such changes are never simply due to error. Joyce's characterisation is exact and consistent, even in the case of minor figures like Stephen's Third Line companions in Clongowes. And, except where symbolic intentions supervene, the characters in the novel regularly correspond to what we know of the personality or function of their real-life counterparts.

There is probably no need to defend a book devoted exclusively to Joyce's schooldays. Herbert Gorman wrote of these as 'the years of his intellectual and emotional development and formation, the creation of the mould, as it were, into which his personality was poured', and judged them to be 'of enormous significance to his career as a man of letters'.[32] Modern psychology would hardly accept such an assessment without further qualification, since it neglects the paramount importance of the very earliest years. But the impact of his Jesuit educators on Joyce's mind and imagination is obvious enough and he was the first to recognise this himself.[33] According to Gorman, 'the four years [sic] at Clongowes may be described as a novitiate, the preparatory training for all that was to follow'.[34] Even after Joyce left his first school:

> it continued to exist in his mind, a vivid reality of sights and scenes and impressions, of legends and dreams and broodings, a sacred place of the coming to consciousness that would be reflected again and again, like sunlight in a shifting mirror, in all the work he would do thereafter.[35]

Clongowes is mentioned by name fifteen times in later chapters of *A Portrait*.[36] In *Ulysses,* apart from the independent reference to Fr Conmee in the 'Wandering Rocks' episode, Stephen's old boarding school comes into his mind at different moments throughout the day.[37] The impact left on his imagination by Belvedere seems to have been less marked.[38] It is a less imposing place and Joyce went there at a less impressionable age. But it undoubtedly helped him to discover and develop his abilities in English, as well as training him in three foreign languages. This was a most important investment for the future. When Joyce told August Suter that, owing to his Jesuit education, 'I have learnt to arrange things in such a way that they become easy to survey and to judge',[39] he is more likely to have had in mind translating Horace for Fr Henry or writing the weekly essay for George Dempsey in Belvedere, than striving with childish eagerness to win first place for the white rose of York in Fr Power's class at Clongowes. It was in Belvedere that Joyce grew towards the intellectual maturity which eventually blossomed into genius. Even his university studies, after Clongowes and Belvedere, were formally under Jesuit direction. But, as Kevin Sullivan has argued, once he left the second school in June 1898, 'his Jesuit education . . . was in reality at an end'.[40]

# ONE

# Clongowes Wood College 1888–91

James Joyce began his schooldays on 30 August 1888 at Clongowes Wood College, the Jesuit boarding school in Co. Kildare.[1] Eoin O'Mahony states that the rector of Clongowes, Fr John Conmee, was Mrs Joyce's 'family friend and possible kinsman'.[2] Fr Conmee and her father John Murray were natives of the neighbouring counties of Roscommon and Longford respectively and some connection between them is possible.[3] In the novels written by John Murray's grandson there are passing indications of more than ordinary familiarity with Fr Conmee. He was to intervene in Joyce's life at school on a couple of memorable occasions.

There is no clear proof of any family connection; anyway Clongowes would have suggested itself to the Joyces without it. Founded in 1814, it was the oldest Catholic lay-school in Ireland and, by reputation, the best.[4] Its aim had been 'the gradual infiltration of the system by highly educated Irish Catholics'[5] and it had already achieved this aim. Fr Henry Lynch, associated with Clongowes since the 1820s, wrote at some time before his death in 1874 that 'certainly it has been always looked on as *much* the most respectable Catholic school in Ireland'.[6] Fr William Delany, already a significant figure in Irish education and afterwards rector of University College, Dublin when Joyce was a student, told Philip Callan MP in 1879: 'Of the

Main entrance and avenue at Clongowes, about 1890.

educational position of Clongowes I need hardly say much to you. Most of our foremost Catholics at the bar and in parliament passed through Clongowes, and many won distinctions in Trinity College'.[7] In the late seventies there was some falling-off in academic standards and Clongowes won only a single exhibition in the first examinations held under the new Intermediate system in the summer of 1879.[8] Other Catholic schools of more recent origin, including its sister-college Tullabeg under the leadership of Fr Delany, did much better in the first years of the new system.[9] But the decline was merely temporary. By the time Joyce went there in 1888, Tullabeg had been amalgamated with Clongowes and the school was entering on a golden period of success in the Intermediate examinations under Fr James Daly. Meanwhile, its standing as the 'best' school in social terms remained unassailed. This was probably of at least equal importance to the Joyces as its reputation for academic endeavour.[10]

Why they should have decided to send him away to school quite so early is difficult to explain. At just over six and a half, he was much the youngest and smallest boy in Clongowes at the time – and possibly in the whole of its long history. He was as much as five and a half years younger than Michael Saurin, one of the boys mentioned in *A Portrait*. Even Tom Furlong, who was no bigger than Joyce when he arrived the following year, was still more than two years older.[11] Joyce's intellectual precocity was very evident in Belvedere. It was less so in Clongowes but may have been sufficient, as Stanislaus Joyce asserts, to persuade the school to receive him six months earlier than the minimum age stipulated in the Prospectus.[12] Ellmann points to the fact that John Joyce had himself been the youngest boy in St Colman's College, Fermoy and 'saw no reason to delay James'.[13] He and Mrs Joyce may have been reassured by what the Prospectus said about the grouping of pupils into three divisions 'to prevent bullying and for the better formation of character', so that a very small boy like James would not be at the mercy of boys much bigger and older than himself.[14] As it was, the boys in his 'line' (as the divisions mentioned in the Prospectus are called in Clongowes) nicknamed him 'Half Past Six' because of his age (probably the subject of frequent interrogation in the first weeks).[15] And he did have to endure some bullying from the likes of 'Nasty' Roche and Wells, who were members of his own line. Considering his size (very evident in the Elements class photograph, 1888–89), these incidents are hardly surprising.

Clongowes has altered somewhat since the Joyces brought their eldest son there at the end of August 1888. The grey mass of the Castle itself, framed by trees at the head of its long avenue of limes, would have caught and held the eye from the moment the car turned in at the imposing, castellated gateway. This building, its compound

Arriving by 'car' at Clongowes, Union Day, 1910.

of styles reflecting something of its chequered history as a sentinel of the Pale, was where the Jesuit community lived.[15a] Then, as now, the school buildings extended southwards to its right. A broad path ran round the other side of the Castle to reveal the great sweep of the playgrounds at the back, skirted by more woods, except to the south east, where the Dublin mountains could be seen in the distance. All this remains as it was and forms the main outline of the place. But there have been considerable additions and modifications to the buildings in the ninety years since Joyce knew them. In front, a new Boys' Chapel (put up in 1907) now rather unhappily dwarfs the Castle and masks the school buildings in front of which it stands. At the back, viewed from the playgrounds, there was a continuous line of buildings in Joyce's time, running from the infirmary away on the left

The west front of the Castle at Clongowes (left) and the old school buildings and former Boys' Chapel (right), taken from the path into the 'pleasure ground', about 1890.

Clongowes from the playgrounds, showing the infirmary, the Carbery Building, the study hall and the east front of the Castle, about 1890.

among the trees, through the 1874 Carbery Building and the study hall, to the east front of the Castle on the right. Since then, the line has been broken by a large new block, dating from 1929 and containing classrooms and dormitories. The Carbery Building, with which it forms a quadrangle, has been completely obscured.

Other sections of Joyce's school have been modified or completely demolished and rebuilt. Of the complex of buildings to the right of the Castle in front, only the present public church (which was then the Boys' Chapel) remains more or less as he knew it. This complex, erected between 1819 and 1821, had been the oldest section of the school apart from the 1818 study hall. It was these buildings which contained the long corridors whose 'troubling odour' Joyce remembered afterwards (421). They formed three sides of a quadrangle, with the original Boys' Chapel on the west. The quadrangle was completed by a wall with an ivy-clad, arched gateway in the middle. This is what the Joyces would have seen on their right as they drove up to the Castle door to be greeted by Fr Conmee. Entirely new buildings now stand on the site and the gateway arch is gone.

The Infirmary, where Joyce began his life in Clongowes, remains as it was, although the school administration currently occupies the ground floor. The swimming bath, entered from just short of the infirmary, is itself unchanged but the area around the bath has been extended – and the water is no longer 'turfcoloured' (263). At right angles to the bath, and entirely hidden from view, stood a structure known (in later times at least) as the 'Wooden Building', which accommodated half a dozen classrooms. This had been put up in a hurry in 1886 to cope with the greatly increased numbers caused by the amalgamation with Tullabeg. Like many such 'temporary' buildings, it continued in use for almost fifty years and was only finally removed to make way for science laboratories in 1966. When little James Joyce was eventually allowed to sleep in a dormitory with the other boys, he was put in the 'top dormitory' in the top storey of the Carbery Building. This still serves as a dormitory for the youngest boys in Clongowes. The study hall building in Joyce's time contained the boys' refectory in its lower storey. (This has now become a school theatre.) It occasionally served that function in his time and he acted there himself. The stairs to the right of the refectory door as you leave it run up past the entrance to 'the low dark narrow corridor' into the Castle, which Joyce had tremulously negotiated on one memorable occasion (301). Although even in his time the smaller boys had a special study of their own,[16] Joyce seems to envisage the big room above the refectory in his description of the study hall in *A Portrait*.

The provisions of Fr Conmee's Prospectus, according to which

# REGISTER of ___ Elements ___ School, from November

| | NAME | RESIDENCE | FIRST FORM — Age at Entrance | FIRST FORM — Date of Entry | SECOND FORM — Days Attended | SECOND FORM — Parent's Name | THIRD FORM — Days Attended | THIRD FORM — Date of Entry |
|---|---|---|---|---|---|---|---|---|
| Rhetoric (m) | Cole Arthur | Carrick-on-Shannon Co Leitrim | | | | Edward Cole | | |
| Poetry | Cole Edward | Do | | " | | Do | | |
| Matric | Cregan Christy | Ludlow St Navan Meath | | | | Joseph Cregan | | |
| I Gram | Delany M.D. | Liberty Hall Arragh | | | | James Delany | | |
| Poetry | Downing G.W.M. | Kenmare Place Killarney | | | | Mrs E. Downing | | |
| III Gram | Ennis Bartholomew | Cellar House Robber Meath | | | | Mr Helena Duffy | | |
| | Furlong Thos C. | 28 Rathmines Road Dublin | | | | Thos J. Furlong | | |
| Rudim | Joyce James A. | 1. Martello Terrace Bray | | | | John Stan Joyce | | |
| Elements | Roch Christopher | 16 Upper Mount St Dublin | | | | George Rochester | | |
| | Kennedy Frederick | 7. Fanchan St Cavan | | | | Hugh P. Kennedy | | |
| | Kickham Rodolph | 28 Upper Gardiner St Dublin | | | | Mrs Mary Kickham | | |

Register of Elements class in Clongowes, 1889–90.

'very young boys' were to enjoy 'special care', were bound to operate in James Joyce's case. According to George Redington Roche, a member of the Higher Line in 1888 (and afterwards rector of Clongowes),[17] Joyce not merely received 'the benefit of female attendance' in the person of Nanny Galvin but was given a room of his own in the infirmary instead of going into the dormitory with the other boys. 'Miss Galvin', according to Sullivan who quotes Roche's evidence, 'was not a trained nurse, but she is reported to have been fully experienced in looking after the ordinary ailments and mishaps of boyhood'.[18] Such an arrangement seems entirely plausible and George Roche is a credible witness. In this way Joyce would have been able to participate in the life of Clongowes apart from the dormitory, with a surrogate mother to comfort him when the rough-and-tumble of an Irish country boarding school became too much for his tender years. Sullivan thinks it possible that special allowance was also made for him in class and that he did not attend study hall at this stage, or at least not regularly.[19] This speculation is apparently not based on George Roche's evidence but on the fact that John Joyce paid a special pension of £25 a year 'to include everything' until September 1890, when the full pension of forty guineas a year became applicable.[20] Sullivan makes the incorrect inference that Joyce remained in the infirmary for the first two years, hence the lower fees.[21] In fact, his name is included in the list of boys in the Third Line top dormitory for 1889–90.[22] The other speculations may be equally mistaken. From half-way through his first year, additional items begin to appear on the account[23] and it is clear that, even in his first year, he was not immune from punishment for misdemeanours in class and around the school.[24] This does not suggest the special treatment Sullivan has in mind. What seems most likely is a gently graduated induction into the ways of the school in the early months, after which he was expected to meet more and more of the demands which applied to the other boys. The process was probably hastened by his obvious ability in class, age and size notwithstanding. And by the end of his first year, at the latest, he had left the security of the infirmary and joined the likes of Thunder, Kickham, MacSwiney, Furlong, Roche and Wells in the dormitory.[25]

The school year in Clongowes got under way only gradually. Despite a warning in the Prospectus about punctuality in returning to school, the boys trickled back day by day over the opening weeks of the term.[26] Fr Daly, the prefect of studies, 'arranged the classes' on 1 September and James Joyce found himself in the 'Class of Elements' with almost forty other boys, many of whom were new arrivals like himself. A week later, after several 'playdays', the retreat began for the upper part of the school. Elements and most of the Third Line

(Rudiments and the younger boys in Third of Grammar) did not follow the main exercises of the retreat but had some class instead. Only on 14 September did 'full schools' begin. Even then, there was an immediate interruption for another playday and 'feast' in the refectory in honour of Clongowes' success in the Intermediate examinations of the preceding summer. While the boys who had distinguished themselves by winning exhibitions and prizes in these exams went on an 'expedition' with Mr Gleeson and another scholastic to Blessington, Joyce and his companions probably went on a walk 'to Major Barton's' (305) or elsewhere in the surrounding countryside, accompanied by one of their masters or the Third Line prefect, Mr Andrew Macardle. Afterwards, dinner (taken at two o'clock) 'lasted an hour'. On Sunday evening during night studies the 'little boys' were brought to join the rest of the school in the big study hall[27] to hear the 'Rules' read out by the minister, Fr Thomas Brown. A few days later, with the evenings drawing in sharply, cricket made way for football on the gravel behind the Castle. The term had begun in earnest.

The reading of the 'Rules' was a long-standing tradition in Clongowes.[28] Even if Fr Brown read rapidly, it must have taken him a considerable time to get through them all. No less than seventy-six rules, covering some twenty-four pages of an octavo notebook, dealt with every aspect of the boys' lives in the school: spiritual duties, the refectory, the dormitory, the study hall, recreation, walks, the swimming bath, the infirmary, the library and private lessons. Finally there were twelve 'general rules' which filled any gaps left by the others. The tone was strict and some of the rules sounded very impressive. Young James, full of 'childish wonder' in those early days (336), must have listened intently as Fr Brown read:

> As Parents have yielded up to the Superiors of this house all authority which nature and Religion have given them over their children, the Boys of the College must remember that it is their duty to respect and revere this authority in their Superiors; hence they are reminded that all acts of insubordination, calumny or detraction against the Superiors, murmuring against their ordinations, groundless complaints, stubbornness and all disrespectful conversations and behaviour are criminal in the sight of God, and directly militate against the 4th commandment.

Joyce probably took little note of the warning against 'groundless complaints' in this rule, but he would have reason to remember it later. At the end of his schooldays, Stephen Dedalus reflects that 'he had never once disobeyed or allowed turbulent companions to seduce him from his habit of quiet obedience' (416). The emphasis on obedience dated from Joyce's earliest contacts with the Jesuits. The next rule said:

> All are clearly to understand that insubordination to anyone placed over them is one of the greatest offences that can be committed by the Boys of this College and they are warned that it will be summarily and severely dealt with nor will any one be kept in the College who persists in making himself troublesome to anyone of his masters or Superiors.

Similarly, the voices which urged Stephen Dedalus 'to be a gentleman above all things and . . . a good catholic above all things' (333) had been heard first by James Joyce in Clongowes. The notion of being a 'gentleman', so dear to his father's heart, was a recurrent motif of the 'Rules':

> All are reminded of the very great importance they should attach to politeness and good manners. Politeness and good manners are absolutely essential for a gentleman and equally so for success in life. Great care should be taken to correct faulty pronunciation, slouching gait – and any other defect of the kind. . . . Politeness requires that all raise their caps when they meet any member of the Community. A gentleman should not require to be reminded of this point of civility. . . . All should be careful to conduct themselves in a gentlemanly manner while outside the College; therefore throwing stones, climbing trees, shouting, whistling and such like are to be avoided. . . . Whistling, romping, and every sort of rude play are prohibited, likewise slang words and all ungentlemanly and unbecoming language. . . . No one must presume to open the desk of another; a breach of this regulation will be considered excessively mean and unbecoming the character of a gentleman.

The final rule, with which the reading ended, was a reminder to the boys that they 'are expected to show on all occasions that they are no less anxious to be good Irish Catholics than they are to acquire knowledge'.[29]

Joyce's companions in Elements in 1888, some thirty-seven in number when they were all there,[30] came from the four corners of Ireland. The majority, however, were from Dublin and the surrounding counties. A photograph of this class has survived, taken with the study hall building and the edge of the Carbery Building in the background. The boys are ranged in three rows, with Fr Power in the centre and James Joyce sitting by himself on the grass in front of the teacher, 'a little boy in a grey belted suit' with 'sidepockets . . . and trousers . . . tucked in at the knees by elastic bands' (344).

The Elements class at Clongowes, 1888–89, with its class master Fr William Power ('Fr Arnall'). James Joyce is by himself on the ground in front. In the back row, Saurin is fourth from the left, Rody Kickham sixth from the left, and Christopher ('Nasty') Roche fifth from the right. In the front row, Wells is second from the right and Francis Pigott fourth from the right.

Underneath, the names have been added in a neat hand, with a few small errors. An informal list of this class is contained in the *Students' Register* 1886–94, which corresponds almost exactly to the names under the photograph. The following is a composite list in alphabetical order:

George Byrne (1887–89) Cork; John Cantwell (1888–89) 12 Wellington Quay, Dublin; Francis Coffey (1889) The Cottage, Mullingar, Co. Westmeath; Edward Costelloe (1888–89) 87 Lr Gardiner St, Dublin; Christopher Cregan (1888–91) Ludlow St, Navan, Co. Meath; James Davys (1888–90 & 1893) Cremona, Swords, Co. Dublin; Gerald Downing (1888–95) Kenmare Place, Tralee, Co. Kerry; Henry Downing (1887–94) Denny St, Tralee; Bartholomew Ennis (1888–94) Cellar House, Nobber, Co. Meath; James Germaine (1889–90) Baltinglass, Co. Wicklow; Gerald Gill (1888–94) and Joseph Gill (1888–93) Roebuck House, Clonskeagh, Co. Dublin; William Hannin (1889 & 1893–94) Banagher, King's Co.; James Joyce (1888–91); Joseph Kelly (1888–90) and Martin Kelly (1888–90) 9 Gresham Terrace, Kingstown; Matthew Kennedy (1889–97) Dublin; Eugene Kenny (1888–89) 77 Merrion Square, Dublin; Edward Keogh (1886–89) 5 Holles St, Dublin; Rodolph Kickham (1888–93) 28 Upper Gardiner St, Dublin; Peter McEleavy (1888–91) Dungannon, Co. Tyrone; Francis McGlade (1888–93) 1 Liscard Terrace, Ormeau Rd, Belfast, Co. Antrim; Augustine McKenna (1888–89 & 1892–94) Woodpark, Clontarf, Dublin; Daniel McLornan (1889–90) Bohil, Dundrod, Crumlin, Co. Antrim; Richard Martin (1889–90) 17 Harcourt St, Dublin; Leo Murphy (1887–92) Woodpark, Glenageary, Kingstown; Arthur O'Connell (1888–94) 49 Lansdowne Rd, Dublin; Edward O'Kelly (1889) Moylough, Co. Galway; Francis Pigott (1887–89) 11 Sandycove Avenue, Kingstown; Christopher Roche (1888–92) 16 Upper Mount St, Dublin; Michael Saurin (1887–93) Harristown House, Hill of Down, Co. Weatmeath; Gerald Scally (1888–90) Deepwell, Blackrock, Co. Dublin; John A. Smyth (1887–93) 17 Wicklow St, Dublin; Robert and Thomas Tighe (1889–96) Claremorris, Co. Mayo; John Verdon (1888–94) and Peter Verdon (1887–?) Rathgar, Dublin; Charles Wells (1888–90) The Cottage, Sandymount Avenue, Dublin.[31]

After the quiet intimacy of Martello Terrace in Bray,[32] James Joyce – like Stephen Dedalus – must have found the experience of being plunged into the middle of all these boys, who 'had all fathers and mothers and different clothes and voices' (252), quite bewildering. Nine of them are named in *A Portrait*. The first mentioned and the most explicitly admired is 'Rody' Kickham, 'a decent fellow'[33] who was good at gravel football, unlike Stephen, and who 'would be

Close-up of James Joyce (from the Elements photograph).

captain of the third line all the fellows said' (246). He also seemed better off than Stephen, with greaves for wearing at football and a hamper in the refectory. In a doodling reverie in Bray on the morning after the Christmas dinner, his is the first name Stephen writes in a list of some of his classmates.[34] Rodolph Kickham in real life sounds not unlike his namesake in the novel. According to *The Clongownian* he was related to Charles Kickham, the author and patriot, and 'was possessed of real literary talents which . . . he does not seem to have developed after leaving school'.[35] He joined the Jesuits in 1895 but left through ill-health after less than two years. (Four of his six brothers were already dead before he left school in 1893.)[36] Subsequently he married and worked a farm in Co. Cork. Shortly before he died, he had written to one of his former teachers, recalling 'the Gravel Football and the Soccer' in Clongowes. *The Clongownian's* obituary remembered how he had 'left from the Lower Line, where he was remarkable not only for his brilliant feats on the Cricket field but also for the sterling qualities of mind and heart which made him so universally popular'.[37]

'Nasty' Roche (whose real name – Christopher – we never hear)[38] was quite unlike Rody Kickham. He was 'a stink'. He had 'big hands' and a loud mouth, and roughly interrogated Stephen about his odd name and what his father was (247). There is a certain crudeness, too, about his question later to Stephen as to whether he really had broken his glasses by accident and his warning that Fr Dolan would be back to pandy him again tomorrow. The Clongowes records tell us very little about parents' professions but they do confirm, more or less, what 'the fellows' said about 'Nasty' Roche's father. He was not a 'magistrate' but a solicitor (252).[39] The personality suggested by entries in the *Punishment Book* corresponds closely to the picture of 'Nasty' Roche in *A Portrait*. Apart from such offences as 'misconduct', 'disobedience', 'constantly late to duties' and the apparently generic 'romping', Christopher Roche was also punished for 'throwing boys into the snow' (with help from three others!), 'rudeness' and more specifically 'calling a boy a vulgar name, "stink"'. The last-named breach of rules occurred on 22 November 1888, not long after he and James Joyce had come to Clongowes. Whether by way of repaying an old injury or not, Joyce has committed the identical offence against Christopher Roche in *A Portrait*, beyond the reach of retribution.

Roche was not the only boy in Clongowes given to vulgar language.[40] The sole reference to 'Cantwell' evokes the robustness of both language and life-style in the Third Line at the end of the eighties:

One day a fellow had said to Cantwell:
   – I'd give you such a belt in a second.
   Cantwell had answered:
   – Go and fight your match. Give Cecil Thunder a belt. I'd like to see you. He'd give you a toe in the rump for yourself.
   That was not a nice expression. His mother had told him not to speak with the rough boys in the college. . . . (247).

Sometimes, however, 'the rough boys' spoke with him. 'Wells' is certainly presented as one of these. Charles Wells in *A Portrait* is the Third Line bully, at least as far as Stephen is concerned. He tries to force him into an exchange of 'his little snuffbox for Wells's seasoned hacking chestnut, the conqueror of forty' and shoves him into the stagnant waters of 'the square ditch' in front of the Castle when he refuses (249).[41] The day afterwards, he continues his persecution of the smallest boy in the line by waiting till the prefect has moved out of earshot in the playroom and then asking him questions designed to embarass him in front of the other boys, about whether or not he kisses his mother at night.[42] When Stephen gets sick as a result of his wetting in the square ditch, Wells in fear appeals to the schoolboy code of which Mr Dedalus had spoken on the day he came to Clongowes – 'never . . . peach on a fellow' (248).[43] Later in the chapter, in the playground conversation about Moonan and Boyle, Wells is the one who turns the discussion round to what will happen to them and gleefully mocks their distress at the prospect of a flogging. In the Elements class photograph, Charles Wells looks like one of the biggest boys in the group. His age is not recorded. Joyce puts him in Third of Grammar but he had only moved up as far as Rudiments when he left Clongowes in 1890.[44] If he was really the bully depicted in *A Portrait*, he seems to have been just as successful in escaping detection on other occasions as with Stephen. His name occurs only twice in the *Punishment Book* and, unless 'romping' on 14 March 1889 refers to some such misdemeanour, he was not caught bullying.

The other member of the 1888–89 class mentioned by his own name is Michael Saurin. He and 'Nasty' Roche 'drank cocoa that their people sent them in tins' because the Clongowes tea was 'hogwash'. 'Their fathers were magistrates the fellows said' (251–52). In Saurin's case, the fellows were quite correct: his father was a Justice of the Peace in Co. Meath.[45]

Joyce mentions by their own names four other boys who were his classmates or at least with him in the Third Line after his first year. Tom Furlong and Anthony MacSwiney, who joined him in Elements (where he was spending a further year) in 1889, are each mentioned once. MacSwiney is merely a name, one of those Stephen writes down on the day after Christmas in Bray.[46] Tom Furlong's voice is heard in class on the day that Stephen was pandied by Fr Dolan, agreeing on request that the prefect of studies would indeed be in again tomorrow. Furlong, although two years older than Joyce, was scarcely bigger than him.[47] They were involved in a number of incidents together. Apart from being caught out of bounds raiding the school orchard, as Ellmann reports,[48] they were also a matching pair of extras in the school play[49] and they shared the altar-serving duties appropriate to their size.[50]

Cecil Thunder was almost certainly not in class with Joyce but they were in the top dormitory together in 1889, when Thunder came to Clongowes.[51] In *A Portrait*, he makes a distinct and not quite flattering contribution to discussions in the playground. He is forthright and not to be trifled with, as Cantwell knew, but there is a touch of schoolboy naïveté about his views. When some of the older boys run away and the Third Line eagerly searches for the latest news of the scandal, Thunder explains confidently that the reason is because they have 'fecked cash out of the rector's room' (283). This is apparently the most awful crime in Thunder's imagination. Wells knows better,

Cecil Thunder (from First Preparatory class photograph, 1891–92).

as he is quick to announce. It is not a matter of stealing, but the much more adult and daring crime of drinking. His hearers would have recalled, at least dimly, what the 'Rules' said about that:

> All are hereby informed that, in order to mark their horror of the vice of intemperance, Superiors have determined that they will at once expel from the College any boy who is found to have brought spirits or other strong drink into it, either for himself or for anyone else – or to have got others to bring it in – or to have partaken of it either *in* the College or *out* of it, or to have it in his possession in any way during the time he is under the authority of the College.[52]

In the event, Wells has to suffer the mortification of hearing his explanation put in the shade by one more sinister still. Cecil Thunder's mind is simpler. When the discussion moves on to the punishment befitting the crime, whatever it was, he gravely opines that flogging is preferable to expulsion because 'a fellow that has been expelled from college is known all his life on account of it' (288). Finally, in the rebellious discussion which follows on Stephen's unjust punishment, Cecil Thunder comes out 'eagerly' with the aged schoolboy chestnut about the teacher not being allowed to lift the pandybat over his shoulder (298).[53] The naïveté properly escapes the other small boys in the Third Line, but it does not escape the reader. Although almost four years older than Joyce and ahead of him in class, Thunder was later his contemporary in UCD,[54] having lost time through his sojourn in the Jesuit novitiate.[55]

Jack Lawton, a Corkman from Midleton, came into Elements in 1890.[56] He was more than a year older than Joyce, who was evidently in the same class, his third successive year in Elements.[57] In *A Portrait,* Jack Lawton and Stephen Dedalus are rivals in class. There were bets in the Third Line 'about who would get first place in elements, Jack Lawton or he' (251). Week by week they alternated in first place. In the arithmetic class, Jack Lawton gets the sum out before Stephen. In the Latin class, when Stephen without his spectacles is *hors de combat,* Lawton is addressed by Fr Arnall (Joyce's name for Fr William Power) as 'the leader of the class' but he does not know the plural of *mare* (291).[57a] In real life, Joyce won the contest in the end. Jack Lawton, whose studies were somewhat interrupted, did not appear in the lists of Intermediate exhibitioners and prizewinners, unlike Joyce, by then in Belvedere. The glimpse of him as a footballer at the beginning of *A Portrait,* his 'yellow boots' dodging out the ball so that 'all the other boots and legs ran after' (248), was a more certain portent of his future at school. Here Joyce offered no competition. In 1898, Lawton played as forward in a famous Clongowes victory in association football over the Leinster Cup-holders, Bohemians, by one goal to nil.[58] His was one of the four names written into his exercise-book at Bray by Stephen Dedalus. By the time Joyce wrote it in *A Portrait,* Jack Lawton was dead.[59]

Apart from these nine boys, given their real names, there are three pseudonymous classmates mentioned in the novel: Simon Moonan, 'Tusker' or 'Lady' Boyle and Fleming. Moonan curries favour with the Third Line prefect, McGlade (Mr Andrew Macardle's fictional counterpart). He tells Rody Kickham not to kick the football after 'all in' 'because the prefect was looking', but one of the other boys dismisses this specious attempt at camaraderie: 'We all know why you speak. You are McGlade's suck' (250). Inside, he playfully knots the false sleeves of the prefect's Jesuit gown behind his back while other boys are talking with him.[60] Later on, with his 'nice clothes' and his present of sweets from the big boys, he is in trouble because of the alleged 'smugging' incident (286). But his name too is inscribed in Stephen's exercise-book in Bray. Boyle's two nicknames derive respectively from an error in class, when he had said elephants had 'tuskers' instead of tusks, and from his effeminate habit of always paring his nails. His name occurs only in relation to the 'smugging' (286). Joyce's reasons for giving both of these boys pseudonyms is clear enough.

24

The Third Line at Clongowes, 1888–89 with their prefect Mr Andrew Macardle ('McGlade'). Joyce is not included, possibly not yet being considered a full member of the Third Line. 'Nasty' Roche and Wells are first and fifth from the left, respectively, on the ground in front.

The reason in Fleming's case is less obvious. Indeed, Fleming is not usually thought to be a pseudonym at all but is taken as referring to Aloysius Fleming from Youghal, Co. Cork (1891–94), the only boy of that name in the *Clongowes Record* whose dates approximate even remotely to those of Joyce.[61] But Aloysius Fleming was sixteen in September 1891, when he came to Clongowes, and he was put into the Matriculation class. He remained there until 1893, when he moved up to First Arts.[62] All this is a far cry from James Joyce, who spent three years in Elements and had just entered Rudiments when he left the school. Stephen Dedalus's 'Fleming' is someone else.

In *A Portrait,* Fleming emerges as Stephen's kindest companion by far. His personal concern, manifested in the two great crises of Stephen's life in Clongowes, make him unique and unlike the other boys, who are either indifferent or actually cruel. He is the one who notices that Stephen is sick and comforts him in the refectory. Stephen reflects that Fleming had been 'very decent to ask him' (252). Fleming too had earlier written a little jingle in the flyleaf of Stephen's geography book – 'for a cod' (255), but in the context the purpose seems to have been in order to make little Stephen laugh and forget his homesickness. In the dormitory, when Stephen wakes up with a fever, it is once again Fleming who notices. He is quick to take responsibility for sending him back to bed and telling the prefect. When Fr Dolan visits the Latin class, Fleming suffers much more severely than Stephen but, as soon as the class ends, he is the first to bring up the subject of the injustice perpetrated against the younger boy. Once again, Stephen is touched by his solicitude and 'felt his heart filled by Fleming's words'. He is unable to reply to 'Nasty' Roche's insensitive query about whether he had told Fr Dolan the truth. Instead, Fleming, who never doubts him, sympathetically answers for him and goes on to make the suggestion on which Stephen eventually acts – to 'go up and tell the rector on him' (297). Fleming is, of course, also the boy who is publicly humiliated in class by Fr Arnall, who dismisses his theme as 'the worst of all' and describes him as 'one of the idlest boys I ever met' (292). He is then cruelly pandied twelve times by Fr Dolan, the prefect of studies. Moreover, this evidently happens frequently to Fleming, so that he has learned to take the precaution of rubbing rosin into his hands. Stephen (who is not quoting what 'the fellows said' in this instance) knows this. It could be argued that this scene and what it implies about Fleming's academic standing in Clongowes is the reason for Joyce's use of a pseudonym. As far as he was concerned, there was no boy of that name in the school in his time and certainly none in the Third Line. But the reason is more plausibly of a quite different kind: the very surprising warmth Joyce shows towards the boy who was Stephen's protector and best friend in Clongowes.

Older boys, who were members of the other lines, would have been remote figures for Joyce and his companions – seen at a distance and only very occasionally encountered in such places as the playground. The line system was designed to ensure separation and it applied everywhere – separate dormitories, libraries and playrooms; separate places in chapel and refectory; separate playgrounds and separate walks on playdays – all under the supervision of a separate prefect for each line. According to the 'Rules', apart from brothers and relations, 'Strict separation of lines must be observed.' This regulation applied even to 'those who cycle round the track during time of recreation'. Ellmann's statement that 'The Third Line included boys under thirteen, the Lower Line boys from thirteen to fifteen, the Higher Line boys from fifteen to eighteen', seems broadly correct.[63] However, age was not the sole criterion and there was always some uncertainty about which line a particular boy ought to be in. Since the age-span in classes was often wide, members of the same class were liable to be in different lines. In *A Portrait,* apart from those already referred to, nine other boys are named or sufficiently specified to have individual identities. These are, in the order in which they are mentioned: Paddy Rath, Jimmy Magee, 'the Spaniard who was allowed to smoke cigars', 'the little Portuguese who wore the woolly cap' (252), Little, Athy, 'Kickham's brother', Corrigan and Dominic Kelly.[64]

Two of these names, Athy and Corrigan, are fictional. Athy is the one of the nine whom Stephen actually meets. This happens first in the infirmary, where Athy is already ensconced when Stephen arrives. He is 'a fellow out of the third of grammar', Stephen knows (263), and as such he could have been a member of the Third Line if he were young enough. The fact that he talks to boys of that line later in the playground would suggest as much but does not prove it. He is privy to a type and an amount of information on that occasion which points to his moving in higher circles, and he is most probably in the Lower Line. He is full of good-natured banter with Brother Michael in the infirmary and he tells Stephen that 'his father kept a lot of racehorses that were spiffing jumpers' (265). Sullivan dismisses Athy as 'an obnoxious goldbrick', in pursuit of his theory that pseudonyms are used only for boys 'who are shown in a really unflattering light'.[65] This theory is mistaken, as the treatment of Fleming clearly shows, and it is hard to see how the verdict on Athy can be justified by the evidence. He is perhaps a little silly, from an adult point of view, but he is harmless and he is quite friendly towards Stephen. Even if 'young Dedalus' was an easily recognisable figure, it is to Athy's credit that, unlike Fr Dolan later, he knows Stephen's name. It is just possible that Athy's remote association with the 'smugging', as the one who seems to know all about the incident, explains his own lack of a real name.[66] This is certainly the reason for Corrigan's pseudonym. He had been directly implicated, according to the rumours in the playground. In the refectory after dinner, Stephen sees him, with his 'big . . . broad shoulders and his hanging black head' (299), leaving with the rest of the Higher Line and he remembers how fat he looked in the swimming bath and how his skin was turf-coloured like the water in the bath. That may have been enough to identify a real boy for Clongownians of the period – but if so, they would have known about the 'smugging' incident in any case, if it actually took place.

Stephen notices Corrigan in the refectory on that occasion only because of the conversation of the Third Liners about him the day before. The other four Higher Line boys he watches coming down the matting in the middle of the refectory had caught his eye on a previous occasion and for less discreditable reasons. Two of them, Paddy Rath and Jimmy Magee, were exceptionally prominent in Clongowes at the time. Paddy Rath, who had come from Tullabeg in 1888, was in First of Grammar when Joyce arrived and, trained in the Tullabeg tradition, he was already a member of the prestigious 'XI', the cricket team in the college. He was elected captain of the house and the cricket XI in 1890–91 and that cricket season was long remembered by Clongownians, chiefly because of his legendary accomplishments. The XI beat all their opponents that summer except Leinster C.C., who were held to a draw. These opponents were not school teams but sides composed of adults, whereas the Clongowes team was all, or almost all, boys. The match against Phoenix, 'practically a Gentlemen of Ireland XI', as Rath himself remarked afterwards,[67] was the most memorable of all. Jimmy Magee wrote his recollections of that match and the 1890–91 season in *The Clongownian* a couple of decades later:

> 1891 was, from a cricketing point of view, the best season the College had in my experience, and the sensational finish of our match that year with Phoenix is likely to be long remembered. The Phoenix had but seven runs to get to win, with four wickets to fall, but our captain, P. M. Rath, agreed to finish the match, and bowling in magnificent form he disposed of these four wickets for two runs, the College thus winning by four runs. Our victories during the season of '91 were, beyond question, attributable to Rath's personality and bowling . . .[68]

The editor of the magazine, Fr Gerald Corr, who had been a Lower Liner at the time, remembered 'how Paddy . . . with his deadly deliveries rattled through those Phoenix wickets, and how, when the last of them had fallen, the whole House rushed forward and "hoisted" our captain'.[69] A few days later, he left Clongowes. Fr

The Clongowes cricket team, 1888–89. Joseph Molony, captain of the school from 1888 until December 1889, is seated in the centre, with his successor Thomas Ross on the right. Paddy Rath, captain in 1890–91, is on the ground (extreme left). George Redington Roche, a later rector of Clongowes, is standing (extreme right).

Henry Fegan, Minister and Higher Line prefect that year, delivered a panegyric of him at tea in the refectory on the evening before his departure, at the end of which Paddy Rath received a great ovation from the boys.[70] Joyce, who 'took a keen interest in cricket',[71] would have been present on these occasions and it is hardly surprising that Stephen should be aware of Paddy Rath. Jimmy Magee succeeded him both as captain of the house and of the cricket XI in 1891–92. He had come to Clongowes in 1889 with his younger brother Louis, who was destined to become one of Ireland's greatest rugby footballers a few years later. Fr Corr remembered how much both brothers had done for that game in Clongowes, introduced in the year of their arrival. He also recalled their prowess as cricketers, 'Jim on several occasions being associated in long partnerships at the wicket with "Ormonde", better known as Fr Gleeson'.[72] In mentioning Rath and Magee, Joyce managed to evoke a whole golden era in the history not only of Clongowes cricket but of the game in Ireland.[73]

29

The other two boys in the Higher Line quartet named by Stephen were bound to linger in his memory, exotic figures in the sometimes grey landscape of an Irish school. 'The Spaniard who was allowed to smoke cigars' was José Araña y Lupardo from Bilbao, who was in Clongowes from 1890 to 1892. 'The little Portuguese who wore the woolly cap' was Francisco da Silva Ruas from Porto, who came in February 1891 and left in 1893.[74] They can both be seen in the Higher Line photograph of 1892, the Portuguese complete with his cap.[75] Louis Magee remembered both of them in an article he wrote for *The Clongownian*, ostensibly about rugby but happily digressing into more general reminiscence. By 1890, rugby in Clongowes was making large strides and some time in the new year a match was played against Presentation College, Cork:

> One of the greatest surprises and successes of the match was a Spaniard named José Araña from Bilbao, in the north of Spain, who played half with me. With the Editor's permission I will digress a little to refer to this great character. This was his first outmatch, and he was not in Clongowes a year at the time. The first day he came he couldn't speak a word of English. I remember sending him up a note in the study that night, which, of course, he couldn't read. After tea, I tried to explain to him what I wrote by using a little bad French and making faces, but it was no use. He had never seen a cricket ball or a football; but before the end of his first year he got his place in the Cricket XI and the Rugby XV, and could tell funny stories – a wonderful performance. In that term also came to the College a little Portuguese chap called Henrico Francisco da Silva Ruas. He was a very funny-looking little fellow, with coal-black hair and yellow face, and wore peculiar yellow-coloured shoes, turned up, and pointed at the toes like a Chinaman's. He ran like a girl in a hobble, and was absolutely useless at games, which, however, he certainly tried to play. José and Henrico, I suppose on account of the natural antipathy of the two races, at first used to scowl at one another, and the Spaniard would laugh at little Henrico's awful attempts to play with the other fellows. They soon, however, became the greatest of friends, and José would make Henrico take some of his 'shop'. The Spaniard was a most original character, extremely handsome, a natural athlete, and always bubbling over with spirits. It was splendid to hear him at times telling of the bull-fights at Bilbao, a sport in the promotion of which his father was interested. Always a very dressy fellow, his collection of neckties had to be seen to be believed. He had I don't know how many boxfuls of them, of all sorts and descriptions. But I fear I have talked more Spanish than football.[76]

The Higher Line at Clongowes, 1891–92 with their prefect Mr Joseph Wrafter. José Araña y Lupardo ('the Spaniard who was allowed to smoke cigars') is fourth from the left in the back row. Francisco da Silva Ruas ('the little Portuguese who wore the woolly cap') is on the extreme left of the row in which Mr Wrafter is sitting.

Louis Magee's digression usefully opens a somewhat larger window on the world Joyce evokes in a few phrases. Their basic accuracy is once more fully confirmed. Araña and Ruas are nameless in *A Portrait* because Joyce as a small boy would hardly have known or been able to remember such complicated names – and Stephen Dedalus can do no better.

Although Joyce does not mention them together, 'Kickham's brother' and Dominic Kelly would have been associated in the popular mind at Clongowes. They were outstanding students in their year, having come from Tullabeg in 1886, and were repeatedly successful in the Intermediate examinations.[77] Both entered the Society of Jesus on the same day, 6 September 1890. Both were in Poetry when Joyce came to Clongowes.[78] It is not for their academic prowess or their Jesuit vocations that they are mentioned in *A Portrait*. Alexander Kickham crops up in a rather peculiar manner in the playground gossip of his younger brother Rody's contemporaries. They are discussing why some of the older boys have run away. Cecil Thunder says it is because they have taken money from the rector's room and when pressed as to who exactly is the culprit directly responsible, he asserts confidently: 'Kickham's brother' (283). Alex Kickham was an unlikely and possibly even absurd candidate for this role, both because of his weak health and his high standing in the school. Moreover, Joyce would probably have known about Kickham's becoming a Jesuit, since this happened while he himself was still in Clongowes.[79] He may intend to further emphasise the naïveté of Cecil Thunder by having him make this assertion, which is dismissed contemptuously by Wells.

Dominic Kelly appears only as an echo in Stephen's reverie about Wells' explanation of the Higher Line scandal: according to this, the culprits had stolen not money from the rector's room but altar wine from the sacristy. Stephen's mind moves from the sacristy to the ceremony of benediction in the chapel, in which he himself took part as a server, and he remembers the time when 'Dominic Kelly sang the first part by himself in the choir' (290). This probably happened quite often. The boys had benediction regularly on Saturdays and Kelly, who was in the choir, was a prominent singer in Clongowes at the time. In the Shrovetide concert in 1890, when he was in his last year at school, he sang 'Kathleen Mavourneen' solo and 'On the blue wave' in a duet with one of the younger boys, Ignatius Little.[80] Joyce, a singer himself (though not in the choir, in his first two years at least), pays tribute to a voice he had admired in school by transcribing Dominic Kelly's name in his novel.[81] The final name of a boy in *A Portrait* is that of Ignatius Little's older brother Stanislaus, whose death and funeral Stephen Dedalus thinks about as he lies sick in the infirmary. This incident will be considered later.

The small boys' dormitory at the top of the Carbery Building in Clongowes, about 1890.

Once the school year got properly under way, with most of the boys back, assigned to their classes and divided into lines, life in Clongowes followed a fairly regular routine. Sundays and special feasts of the church, as well as playdays and 'half-evenings', modified the order of time. But on ordinary days, designated *de more* in the Higher Line *Prefect's Journal*,[82] it followed a pattern discernible in Joyce's account. The boys rose at 6.30 at the sound of a bell and, in the dormitory at the top of the Carbery Building where Joyce was from at least the end of his first year, washed in the basins which stood at the foot of each curtained bed. Then they came down the stairs and turned left at the end of the bottom corridor of the 'new building', as the Carbery was still known, to go by the long gallery to the chapel for morning prayers and Mass. The chapel was on the right, off the far end of this gallery, and was entered (as it still is today) by a door at the side of the altar. The sacristy was on the other side. After Mass, they returned by the same gallery and, instead of turning right at the end and back into the Carbery Building, they went left through the short gallery and then right, past the foot of the stairs, to the refectory for breakfast.[83]

This was one of three main meals a day in Joyce's time – the midday lunch referred to in the timetable was possibly too perfunctory to be worth mentioning and neither he nor others writing of this period speak of it. School food has always been notorious, at

The long gallery at Clongowes, about 1890. The Higher Line and Lower Line playrooms and libraries are on the left and the 'magazine' and the entrance to the 'Square' on the right. At the far end the short gallery (left) meets the bottom of the Carbery Building (right).

The refectory at Clongowes, about 1890. Joyce took part in theatricals here at Easter 1891.

Playroom at Clongowes, 1910. This was the Third Line playroom in Joyce's day.

least among the boys, and Stephen's experience of the Clongowes food in the eighties and nineties runs true to type. Hence we hear of 'the two prints of butter on his plate' (251) and the 'junks of white damp bread' (S 165), the tea which some of the boys could not drink because they said it was 'hogwash' (252), 'beef fringed with green fat like blubber' (S 165), 'the blackish fish fritters they got on Wednesdays in Lent' and the potato which had 'the mark of the spade in it' (298), and the Friday pudding which 'Nasty' Roche called 'dog-in-the-blanket' (247). Other Clongownians, before and after Joyce, confirm this picture of what the basic school menu contained.[84] Louis Forrest, writing in *The Rhetorician* in the spring of 1888, anticipated 'Nasty' Roche's sentiments when he referred to 'that watery beverage flattered by the name of tea'.[85] In the refectory, over which the minister presided,[86] the Higher Line sat at the top, the Lower Line in the middle and the small boys nearest the door. To the right of the door sat a special category, the Intermediate exhibitioners, who received special fare as a reward for their scholastic attainments and, no doubt, an incentive to others. Joyce was too young to contend for a place at what the rest of the school called 'the pigs' table'.[87]

After breakfast the boys were free until study, followed by two hours of class. The small boys had a special study, which was probably on the ground floor of the Carbery Building. Their classes were held either on this corridor or in the now vanished Wooden Building. This was reached by going along the corridor towards the infirmary and turning right beyond the swimming bath. After the midday break, there were two more classes in the afternoon from one o'clock till three, then 'washing' and dinner at three-thirty.[88] The boys were free from the end of dinner until beads in the chapel at five-fifteen. Then they went to study again until supper at seven. The small boys went to bed after night prayers, which were said in the chapel at eight-fifteen.

Depending on the time, the season and the weather, recreation on ordinary days was spent either in the playgrounds, when it was 'all out', or, when it was 'all in', in playrooms and libraries of the different lines. The Third Line recreation rooms in Joyce's time were off the short gallery on your right as you came round the corner from the refectory. They looked across the old quadrangle to the chapel on the other side. Stephen is sitting in the playroom after supper one evening, 'pretending to watch a game of dominoes' (253), when Wells comes up to catechise him about kissing his mother. There was a door to the playground just across the short gallery from these rooms, leading straight out to the wide space between the Castle and the Higher Line cricket ground. This is where the Third Line played in the winter, so that Stephen can easily see the lights in the Castle in the

October dusk, as he half-heartedly joins in gravel football.

Recreation, and the boys' life in school outside class, was under the supervision of the line prefects. The Higher Line Prefect had authority over the other two and it is his cry of 'all in!' on the playground which gives the signal to them for the end of recreation (249). Stephen Dedalus has a prefect called McGlade, identified as Mr Andrew Macardle in real life. James Joyce had three different Third Line Prefects: Macardle in 1888–89, Mr Thomas Murphy in 1889–90 and Mr Henry Potter after that. But only Macardle, under his pseudonym, appears in *A Portrait*. Andrew Macardle, a northerner,[89] is quite favourably portrayed in the novel, where he is a benign if shadowy presence. He is glimpsed on the football ground and in the playroom.[90] Once it has been established that Stephen's illness is genuine, his prefect tries to cheer him up by making a joke about 'the collywobbles'. Even though he is shivering too much to laugh, Stephen reflects that 'he was very decent to say that' (263) – and we recognise in the word the Victorian schoolboy's supreme accolade.[91] Macardle may owe his inclusion in the book to the fact that he was James Joyce's first prefect and, as such, likely to have made a bigger impact than his successors. His role may have been all the more important because of his charge's extreme youth and special status in his first year.[92]

These factors, however, did not prevent Macardle from sending Joyce for punishment on at least two occasions – both of them in March 1889.[93] On the first, Joyce was given six for 'wearing boots in the house'. This was a breach of the rule which stated:

> All must change their boots as soon as they come from the play-ground into the house. House shoes must never be worn on the play-ground and it is strictly forbidden to wear spiked boots in the play-rooms, and much more in the libraries or refectory.

Joyce's account in the *Ledger* for the half-year from February includes five shillings for 'slippers', presumably the equivalent of 'house shoes', for which he paid the same amount on two subsequent occasions in each of the succeeding years.[94] On 14 March Mr Macardle sent him for four for, in his case, the astonishingly portentous offence of 'vulgar language'. This too was a breach of the 'Rules', which prohibited 'slang words and all ungentlemanly and unbecoming language'. On the basis of Christopher Roche's punishment earlier in the year, also at Mr Macardle's behest, for 'calling a boy a vulgar name "stink" ', it is possible to speculate about the vulgarity uttered by the seven-year-old James Joyce.[95] Mr Macardle had no idea of what this smallest boy in his care would one day be capable of in the matter of vulgar language. Judged by the portrayal of McGlade in his novel, Joyce

| Date | NAME | Punishment | Offence | |
|------|------|-----------|---------|---|
| | G. Gill | 6 | Talking in class | A. Mac... |
| | F. Coffey | 6 | Constantly talking & playing i class | " |
| 14th March | F. McGlade | 2 | | " |
| " | G. Scally | " | Going out of bounds | " |
| " | Jn Gill | " | | " |
| " | J. Colgan | 12 | Bath without leave | " |
| " | D. Downing | 10 | Talking in Square | " |
| " | C. Eardley | 18 | " | " |
| " | C. Wells | 6 | Romping | " |
| " | J. Joyce | 4 | Vulgar language | " |
| " | C. Roche | 10 | Constantly late to duties | " |
| " | A. O'Kelly | 4 | Out of bounds | " |
| 19th " | C. Roche | 6 | Rudeness | " |
| " | J. Colgan | 9 | Opening another boy's desk | Jeffcoat |
| " " | E. Costello | 9 | Lessons | Gwynn |
| 'o th " | J. Colgan | 8 | Lessons | McCorm... |
| " | H. George | 6 | Lessons not known | Jeffcoat |
| " | J. Lynch | 9 | Not Knowing Virgil | Gleeson |
| " | Wm Hannin | 6 | Idling | Macard... |

The *Punishment Book* for 14 March 1889.

does not seem to have borne a grudge against the Third Line Prefect of 1889.

This was not Joyce's only contact with Mr Macardle. He taught Elements arithmetic in 1888–89 and had Joyce's class again the following year, probably for the same subject. In addition he was Elements class-master in that year. The function of the class-master as it operated fifteen years later was subsequently described in the school magazine. It is unlikely to have changed much, if at all, from Joyce's time:

> Priest or scholastic he took his class for Latin and Religious Knowledge, gave us a 'spiff' on Saturdays if entreated (morals and manners came into it), took us out on walks and distributed letters. More than that, in a special way he was friend and counsellor of the class, its advocate in trouble. . . .[96]

In *A Portrait,* however, McGlade does not feature as a teacher and Stephen Dedalus does 'sums' with Fr Arnall (250). During his time in Clongowes, Joyce's class masters were as follows: Fr William Power in 1888–89, Mr Macardle in 1889–90, Mr Patrick Barrett in 1890–91 and, for the time that he seems to have returned at the start of the next academic year, Mr James Jeffcoat. These are the only ones among his teachers who appear in *A Portrait.* Mr Macardle is McGlade, Mr Barrett keeps his own name, Fr Power is Fr Arnall and Mr Jeffcoat is Mr Harford.

Unlike Macardle, the other two scholastics are mentioned only in passing. Jeffcoat, disguised as Harford, teaches writing. 'All the other masters got into dreadful waxes', but 'Mr Harford was very decent and never got into a wax'. We see him moving quietly among the class, helping them with their writing and 'sometimes sitting with the boy to show him how to hold his pen' (290). James Jeffcoat was not yet twenty-two when he arrived in Clongowes in the same year as Joyce, to begin five years of teaching. He was an Englishman who had been born a Protestant of indeterminate sect. He first adhered to Anglicanism and then, at the age of sixteen, became a Catholic in 1882. He joined the Irish Jesuits a year later.[97] Sullivan suggests that his gentleness in the writing class may be the patience and idealism of the new teacher in his first year.[98] Quite the reverse seems to have been true. He does not appear to have had Joyce's class at all in his first year, when he was class-master for Rudiments. Judging from the *Punishment Book,* they gave him a lively time and his name appears more often than any other master except one. Boys were sent from his class for such interesting offences as 'playing in class' (thirteen times), 'humming in class', 'putting paper into ink-wells', 'striking matches in class', 'firing slap bang in class' and 'throwing things about the

The Clongowes community, 1889–90. The rector, Fr Conmee, is seated in the centre, with the minister Fr Henry Fegan second from left. At the back are Mr Barrett (extreme left), Mr Gleeson (fifth from left), Mr Francis Ryan, who taught Joyce in Belvedere and is mentioned in *Dubliners* (seventh from left), Mr Macardle (fourth from right) and Mr James Jeffcoat ('Mr Harford', third from right). Fr Daly ('Fr Dolan') and a number of others are not in the photograph.

room'. After this difficult first year, he seems to have gained control. His name does not appear at all for the rest of his time in Clongowes.[99]

Mr Barrett keeps his own name. Stephen, in his reveries, thinks of him as 'Mr Barrett' early on (271) but later more familiarly as 'Paddy Barrett' (292), a subtle indication of the boy's growing assurance. As 'Mr Barrett', he administers a pandybat, which he calls a 'turkey', as Stephen remembers on Christmas Day (271). Later, Wells refers to him as 'old Barrett', whose 'new way of twisting the note so that you can't open it and fold it again to see how many ferulae you are to get' he describes indignantly in the Third Line playground (287). Once again, Joyce's memory is quite accurate and no detail in his brief description appears fortuitous. Mr Barrett was in Clongowes for four years, from 1889 to 1893. In his first year he was Gallery Prefect, a job which involved general supervision about the school and included the administration of punishment. In his second year he became Elements class-teacher and in this capacity would have been writing notes and sending boys out to be pandied by someone else.[100]

But the teacher most vividly described in *A Portrait* is Fr William Power. As Fr Arnall, he teaches 'sums' and Latin. In the arithmetic class, he uses the method of 'emulation' recommended by the *Ratio Studiorum*,[101] dividing them into two rival camps, Lancaster and York. We hear him urging the two sides on: 'Now then, who will win? Go ahead, York! Go ahead, Lancaster! ... Bravo Lancaster! The red rose wins. Come on now, York! Forge ahead!' Stephen notes that 'Fr Arnall's face looked very black, but he was not in a wax: he was laughing' (250–51). In the Latin lesson, later in the year, he is not laughing: 'His face was very black looking and his eyes were staring though his voice was so quiet'. He shouts at Fleming on account of his bad theme, and Stephen, 'glancing timidly at Fr Arnall's dark face, saw that it was a little red from the wax he was in' (292). The impression we receive, filtered through the child's perceptions, is of a man of volatile temperament, whose almost childish enthusiasms can give way unexpectedly to angry moods.

The real-life counterpart of Arnall, Fr William Power, had already spent seven years in Clongowes. After five years as a scholastic between 1870 and 1875, he had returned as a priest to be the teacher of Third of Grammar in 1882–83. Having taught in several other schools, he came back in 1887 as teacher of Rudiments, dropping down to Elements the following year. He was forty at the time. He is remembered in the Irish province as a colourful eccentric; many who are still alive knew him in his old age in Tullabeg. Before moving there in 1900, he had been transferred continually from school to school. After leaving Clongowes in 1889 he taught in four different Australian schools in less than six years. The impression of instability, an inability to settle anywhere, is accurate.[102] He was sent back to Clongowes in 1896 as teacher of Rudiments and managed to stay four years this time. But in 1900 he went into virtual retirement in Tullabeg, where he spent the rest of his long life.

Joyce's picture of Fr Arnall corresponds closely with the memories of those who knew Fr Power. *The Clongownian* obituary recalled his distinctive teaching methods:

> Those who were in his classes, whether in Tullabeg or in Clongowes, will remember how he stimulated the interest of the boys in their work by dividing the class into two rival camps of Romans and Carthaginians, pitting one against the other and awarding or deducting marks according as lessons were known or

Fr William Power and the Rudiments class at Clongowes, 1887–88, with their 'York' and 'Lancaster' banners.

missed. How keen was the rivalry between the camps, how eagerly each side watched for a mistake, with its accompanying loss of marks, to be made by the other, and what angry looks and muttered threats greeted him, who by a mistake in gender or declension or conjugation, risked the loss to his side of the much coveted tin of biscuits.[103]

The reference to Romans and Carthaginians might suggest that Joyce's memory had let him down or that some ulterior motive, symbolic perhaps, had led him to adjust the facts slightly. Not so. It was common to use the Punic Wars as a model and William Delany, under whom Power had taught, certainly did so in Tullabeg.[104] Perhaps Mr Power did the same at that time, but in Clongowes he made a change. A damaged photograph of his 1887 Rudiments class survives, complete with the banners of Lancaster and York, to prove the veracity of Joyce.[105] Fr Cyril Power (no relation), who was a novice in Tullabeg from 1907 to 1909, remembered his namesake as 'kindly' but 'a child, who never grew up'.[106]

Ironically, perhaps, it is William Power, in the guise of Fr Arnall, who comes to epitomise the betrayal of childhood in the life of Stephen Dedalus, first in Clongowes and later in Belvedere. Joyce uses the name of Arnall for the fear-inducing preacher of the retreat in Stephen's second school. This was not William Power,[107] but Joyce has a symbolic reason for identifying the two. In Clongowes Fr Arnall is the object of Stephen's most naïve and childish submission to the wisdom and prestige of the Church. 'Fr Arnall knew more than Dante', he thinks early in his schooldays, 'because he was a priest' (249). Later, when Fr Arnall is obviously angry in the Latin class, Stephen muses: 'Was that a sin for Father Arnall to be in a wax or was he allowed to get into a wax when the boys were idle because that made them study better or was he only letting on to be in a wax? It was because he was allowed, because a priest would know what a sin was and would not do it' (292). His trust is bitterly betrayed. Fr Arnall does not save him from unjust punishment by the prefect of studies. He is not only physically but emotionally crushed: 'scarlet with shame' (296) he goes back to his place, a leader of the class reduced to the same category as Fleming. The same complex of emotions – trust, the sense of betrayal, and the revelation of what he sees as his own gullibility, leading this time to complete rejection – will be associated with the Belvedere retreat. Fr Arnall's name is appropriate.[108]

About what William Power and his colleagues actually taught Joyce, we know very little. Sullivan has studied the evidence of *A Portrait* and noted the six subjects it refers to: spelling, sums,

The study hall at Clongowes, about 1890.

geography, writing, Latin and history.[109] In 1888–89 Power taught
Latin and spelling and Mr Macardle taught arithmetic.[110] Who
taught the other subjects we do not know. After 1889, apart from the
subjects taught by the class-master and the fact that Mr Barrett had
Joyce's class in 1889–90,[111] we have no idea who his masters were or
what they taught. It is probable, of course, that most of the teaching
was done by the class-master. Some thirty years earlier, the following
general instructions for Elements were issued by the Prefect of
Studies:

> The chief duty is [to] teach the little children to spell, read and
> know their chatechism [sic] – it is impossible to determine the
> matter – if some are much better than others, the school might be
> divided and sub-divided. Let each get all he can – much attention
> ought be paid to their manners in class – they retain any impres-
> sion that is made on them.[112]

The Intermediate, introduced twenty years after the above was
written, must have modified even the syllabus of Elements. The
problem referred to here still existed: boys often stayed back in the

same class and Joyce spent as many as three years in Elements. Sullivan supplies specific items from the matter of an examination in religious knowledge which 'Joyce and his classmates in the Lower Line' supposedly sat in December 1890.[113] But the syllabus from which he draws the information is specifically for Junior Grade, Middle Grade and Senior Grade classes, in other words for the boys at the top of the school. Joyce was not to reach the lowest of these until 1894 in Belvedere. And he was, of course, never in the Lower Line at Clongowes. All we can be fairly sure of is that he was taught religious knowledge by each of his class-masters in turn. Overall, he may have been one of the leaders in his class, like Stephen Dedalus, at least towards the end of his time. But Kevin Sullivan's verdict on Joyce's academic record as a small boy in Clongowes is probably correct: 'The memory . . . is of a small boy "more delicate than brilliant" who, however innately gifted, made no remarkable display of those gifts during his three and a half years at the college.'[114]

Joyce does not refer to religious instruction in *A Portrait*, but the central place of religion in the life of the school is very evident. There are references in the novel to such regular features as Mass and night prayers, benediction and confession, seasonal events like the observance of Lent and 'the procession to the little altar in the woods' (284) on the feast of the Sacred Heart in June,[115] and special

Classroom at Clongowes in the bottom corridor of the Carbery Building, a little after Joyce's time (about 1910). The blackboard is headed 'A.M.D.G.'

The Boys' Chapel at Clongowes about 1890. The door from the long gallery is on the left of the altar and the sacristy is on the right.

occurrences like his own first holy communion and the funeral rites of a boy who had died. In the 'Rules', pride of place was given to 'spiritual duties' and the boys' behaviour in the chapel and elsewhere on these occasions was laid down with the most minute care:

> All are to attend regularly at morning and evening Prayers, Mass, Beads, and all other spiritual duties with attention and devotion. At all times religious silence should be observed in the Chapel; and looking round, lounging on the benches, or any unbecoming posture, should be carefully avoided. . . .
> On Confession days no one should presume to approach the Sacred Tribunal without at least a quarter of an hour's preparation. Silence and decorum should be observed in the Gallery going to and coming from Confession . . .

And so on. The religious awe of Stephen Dedalus when he tries to imagine some of the senior boys entering the sacristy to steal altar-wine is more intelligible against the background of the 'Rules'.[116] They also insisted that 'To prevent inattention during Mass and

Benediction each one should have his prayer-book'. This had evidently not been anticipated by the Joyces, but the omission was duly made good some time during their son's first year in Clongowes. The occasion was almost certainly his first holy communion, which usually took place at the beginning of June.[117] According to his own reference in *A Portrait*, the rector, Fr Conmee, celebrated Mass that morning.

The Boys' Chapel, in which the seasons and major feasts of the Church's year were solemnly observed, was remembered by a Clongownian of slightly later vintage than Joyce:

> For four years I worshipped in the Boys' Chapel, homely because it was small and 'intimate' in that we could hear and see everything and the preacher could almost converse with us. In those days the communion rails began at the four pillars slightly behind the altar where it is now, but was then five or six yards farther back, and the sanctuary much more impressive. Unforgettable were the Holy Week ceremonies seen at close quarters (we spent Easter here!) especially the tenor voice of Father Elliot ringing out in the *Exultet*. In this way the riches of the Church's Liturgy were brought home to us for the first time. . . .[118]

Here, Joyce not only attended Mass and the other ceremonies regularly but also took part, in benediction at least, as a server. He himself refers to being 'dressed as boatbearer' (284) to assist in the procession for the feast of the Sacred Heart in June. As Sullivan remarks, this was 'an office that always devolves on tiny fellows' and he was an obvious choice for it.[119] He served regularly at benediction (and not just on special occasions like the procession) from his first year in Clongowes.[120]

As was logical, he shared his duties with the second smallest boy in the school, Tom Furlong, who had come to Clongowes in 1889. They were evidently capable of combining forces off the altar as well as on it, as an intriguing entry in the *Minister's Journal* for Thursday 22 May 1890 shows. Each year, in addition to their other privileges, the exhibitioners in Clongowes were given a half-day and a feast in May. Certain other boys were allowed to join in all or part of these festivities. Unfortunately, it was not quite clear who qualified and who did not and each year boys capitalised on the confusion to urge their claims. Fr Fegan, the minister, sought to preclude further confusion by making the following entry:

> Exhibitioners, Choir, Rhetoric, Gamekeepers and Shopkeepers got half day (free after 12.30 lunch for them). They dined in Refectory at 5.20 – had coffee after dinner. Went to prayers with the rest. No

47

The Clongowes exhibitioners, 1888–89 with Mr James O'Dwyer. Alexander Kickham ('Kickham's brother') and Dominic Kelly are on the ground in front. Tim Corcoran and Thomas Emerson, staff-members of *The Rhetorician*, are seated second from the left and extreme right respectively.

smoking allowed. Besides the above the Thurifer, 1st and 2nd Acol(yte) were free. All the [*gap in text*] got to the feast at 5.20. The 2 small boys of the III Line for the few minutes work on Saturday Evenings claimed the feast and half-day. They also claimed during the term to be allowed in to the Choir feasts, but

1   They were forbidden the choir feasts
2   They did not get the half-day
3   They *were* let in to the feast but told that it would not again be allowed. They come to 2nd table on Saturday Evgs and get some little thing extra – that is all, and sufficient for their work.[120a]

Fr Fegan was a legendary figure in Clongowes. He had held the office of Higher Line Prefect in the difficult year of the amalgamation with Tullabeg[121] and held it again, without ceasing to be minister, in 1890–91. But he was not proof against the entreaties of the most diminutive members of the Third Line and, on this occasion, Furlong and Joyce rejoiced![122]

Games in Clongowes were already well organised in James Joyce's time. The two principal games were gravel football and cricket, both of which feature in the Clongowes chapter of *A Portrait*. Indeed, it begins with one and ends with the other. The year began with cricket but this made way for football by the end of September and did not resume till after Easter.[123] In between, gravel football held sway. Its season culminated in the 'Grand Match' by which 17 March was traditionally celebrated. On this occasion the rector (unathletic Fr Conmee) 'kicked off' in the Higher Line, the minister in the Lower Line and 'some other government representative' in the Third Line. This game, now quite defunct, had been introduced from Stonyhurst, the Jesuit college in Lancashire. Apart from Tullabeg prior to the amalgamation of 1886, it was played only in Clongowes. It bore a broad resemblance to soccer, but the ball (small, hard, not perfectly spherical and made on the premises) could be struck by the closed hand ('boxed') when in flight. The goals were two sets of uprights, 'fresh from the primeval forest', with no cross-bar, placed at diagonal corners of the playing area. It could be played by large numbers and for several hours at a time. It got its name from the gravel surface on which it was always played. Unless the rules regulating tackling were strictly observed, it was liable to degenerate into 'a lawless scramble . . . where almost anything was allowed except carrying the ball'. This is what was beginning to happen in Joyce's time. According to Stanislaus, his brother did not enjoy the game any more than Stephen Dedalus.[124] He spends his time 'on the fringe of his line, out of sight of his prefect, out of the reach of the rude feet, feigning to run now and

Gravel football at Clongowes, December 1910. Note the posts, with no cross-bar, in the upper left-hand corner. The photograph was taken by Dominic Kelly, by then a member of the Jesuit community in Clongowes.

then' (246). Rugby football, which gave a central place to carrying the ball, was introduced after the amalgamation and it quickly made strides. The first rugby match against outside opponents (or 'outmatch') was played against Lansdowne in March 1889.[125] Games were subsequently played against Lansdowne and two other Dublin clubs, Wanderers and Bective Rangers.[126] According to *A Portrait*, on one occasion the visitors from Bective brought a present of 'a ball of creamy sweets' in the club colours of red and green for their hosts. That evening, in the refectory, 'the fellows of the football fifteen' had transferred the gift to well-dressed Simon Moonan of the Third Line, by rolling it to him down the carpet (286). This is Joyce's only reference to rugby, which quickly replaced gravel football and has remained the principal sport in Clongowes ever since.

Easter, when there was a mere four days' break from study (Holy Saturday until Easter Tuesday inclusive), was traditionally marked by holding athletic sports.[127] Stanislaus reports that Joyce was good at these and brought home trophies.[128] He himself depicts Stephen 'walking about the grounds watching the sports in Clongowes and eating slim jim out of his cricket cap' (417). John Horgan recounts a story that Joyce 'played Spillikins with great ability'.[129] It is difficult to ascertain what 'Spillikins' was. But it may have been one of the games – like stilts, tops and rounders – which occupied the interval between the end of gravel football and the start of cricket.[130] It is thus in late March or early April that the playground discussion concerning scandal in high places is held:

> ... there was no play on the football grounds for cricket was coming: and some said that Barnes would be prof and some said it would be Flowers. And all over the playgrounds they were playing rounders and bowling twisters and lobs. And from here and from there came the sounds of the cricket bats through the soft grey air (285).

(Barnes and Flowers were cricket professionals, both from Nottingham, who came over to coach in Clongowes each summer from 1888 to 1891).[131] Cycling too is in vogue at this time of year. Stephen has just been knocked down by one of the 'sprinters' on the cinderpath. Cycling had been recently introduced and the track, running round the perimeter of the Higher Line cricket ground, had been laid down about the time of the amalgamation.[132] When the cricket season began, 'the XI' played a series of out-matches against opponents from the Curragh Brigade, the Dublin Garrison, Phoenix, Leinster, Naas and Co. Kildare and the Clongowes 'Past'.[133] In Joyce's time Clongowes cricket was of a very high standard and these

'The fellows of the football fifteen', 1891–92. Louis Magee, brother of Jimmy, and later one of Ireland's greatest rugby footballers, is seated on the ground in front of the player holding the ball.

Cricket practice in the Lower Line at Clongowes, about 1912.

matches generated great excitement.[134] Stanislaus says that his
brother played the game and showed promise as a bat.[135] But in *A
Portrait* the image of Stephen as intellectual and uninvolved is set from
the beginning.

John Horgan recalled 'the Clongowes of the nineties . . . warm
summer afternoons punctuated by the click of bat on ball; long walks
on winter "play days" through the flat, wooded countryside to nearby
villages or places of historic interest, followed by a plunge into the
warm turfcoloured water of the swimming bath . . .'[136] Stephen
Dedalus also knew 'the sound of the cricket bats . . . like drops of
water in a fountain falling softly in the brimming bowl'. He
remembered the countryside around Clongowes 'when they went out
for a walk to Major Barton's' (305), accompanied by their class-
master.[137] He was familiar too with 'the warm moist air, the noise of
plunges, the smell of towels, like medicine' (263) and 'the
turfcoloured bogwater in the shallow end of the bath' (299–300)
where the small boys went.[137a] And Joyce would also have remembered, though he does not mention it in *A Portrait*, another extra-
curricular activity – Fr William Power's drill sessions. The *Punishment
Book* contains an entry for 11 December 1889 showing that five of his
classmates, including Roche and Kickham, were sent for two each by
Fr Power on account of unspecified misdemeanours at 'drill'. There is
a photograph in an early issue of *The Clongownian* of the Rudiments
class on parade. They stand to attention, eyes left to face the camera,
complete with military sashes and imitation rifles, under the
command of their top-hatted drill sergeant.[138]

The choir at Clongowes, 1888–89, with Dominic Kelly, who 'sang the first part by himself' at benediction, in the middle row, second from the right.

The swimming bath at Clongowes about 1890. Through the door, the corridor leading right to the infirmary can be seen.

In his final full year in Clongowes Joyce took piano lessons, as the *Ledger* shows.[139] He does not mention this himself. Nor does he mention what may have made a bigger impression on him, the Easter play of 1891 produced by one of the prefects, Mr Joseph Wrafter.[140] This was a burlesque called 'Aladdin, or The Wonderful Scamp', a change from the Shakespeare plays more usual in Clongowes at the time.[141] In the decorative programme printed for the occasion, the names of Paddy Rath and the Magee brothers are to be noticed among the principals. The only one of Joyce's classmates with a main part was Arthur O'Connell. But several other Third Liners were involved as extras, denominated as 'courtiers, attendants, imps, etc.' These included Cecil Thunder, Jack Lawton, Tom Furlong and Joyce himself. A photograph survives, showing most of the principals in front and twelve of these extras at the back.[142] The two smallest boys in Clongowes are easily recognisable at either end of the back row, Joyce on the left and Furlong (looking, if anything, even smaller) on the right. The play was staged in the refectory, which was cleared for the occasion, and started at 8.30. Guests had been invited from

# ALADDIN,

## Or THE WONDERFUL SCAMP.

### A BURLESQUE.

THE SULTAN (a Monarch in difficulties) ... WILLIAM J. GRANT

THE VIZIER { who, amidst other dirty work, is supposed to have cleaned out the Exchequer. } HENRY HARRINGTON

PEKOE (the Vizier's hope and his own pride) ... LOUIS M. MAGEE

ALADDIN ... .. ... GEOFFREY GRATTAN ESMONDE

ABANAZAR (a Magician) ... ... ... JAMES M. MAGEE

THE SLAVE OF THE LAMP ... ... ... JAMES J. CLARKE

THE GENIUS OF THE RING ... ... ... PATRICK M. RATH

THE WIDOW TWANKAY { Aladdin's mother, "who," to quote 'he 'Arabian Nights,' "was rather old and who even in her youth had not possessed any beauty. } GEOFFREY J. GILL

PRINCESS BADROULBOUDOUR (the Sultan's Daughter)

ARTHUR P. O'CONNELL

MANDARINS.—James Fegan, Joseph McArdle, Daniel Sweeney, William Mooney, Jeremiah O'Neill, Thomas O Brien, Philip Redmond, Joseph Carvill, Hugh Sheridan, Patrick Gallagher.

COURTIERS, ATTENDANTS, IMPS. &c.—William L. Murphy, Francis McGlade, Dominic Hackett, Matthew Kennedy, Patrick Field, Lewis Comyn, John McSweeney, Cecil Thunder, Gerald Gill, Gerald Downing, John Verdon, Charles Holohan, William Hackett, Vincent Kennedy, James Joyce, Thomas Furlong, William Field, John Lawton, Thomas Fitzgerald.

The programme for 'Aladdin, or The Wonderful Scamp', produced at Clongowes, Easter 1891. James Joyce, along with Cecil Thunder, Thomas Furlong and 'Jack' Lawton, are among the 'Courtiers, Attendants, Imps, etc.' listed at the end.

The cast of 'Aladdin, or The Wonderful Scamp'. James Joyce is in the back row, extreme left. Thomas Furlong is at the other end of the row.

The 'square ditch' at Clongowes, with the former Boys' Chapel in the upper left-hand corner: 'How cold and slimy the water had been!'

Close-up of Charles Wells (from the 1888–89 Elements photograph): 'He did not like Wells's face. It was Wells who had shouldered him into the square ditch'.

Dublin and one of them, a recent past pupil, William Butler, wrote a review for *The Rhetorician*. According to him, it was an excellent production:

> It was distinguished by some capital songs arranged to popular airs and very well rendered; the comic scenes left nothing to be desired; whilst the scenery and dresses were of the most gorgeous description. The stage machinery worked admirably and the sudden change from the glittering cave of the magician to Aladdin's humble abode was excellently done. The songs were retouched for the occasion by the Rector and enlivened by local allusions. They took very well, especially various duets between Aladdin and his doating mother, the widow Twankay. [143]

One feature of 'Aladdin', typical of these Victorian burlesques, may have appealed especially to James Joyce:

> The piece, of course, contains a large number of hideous puns. We will only inflict one on our readers. Pekoe begs the Princess to quaff a tea-cup with him to their happy union, and she retorts with withering scorn: 'I don't teak up with such as you.' [144]

The Clongowes chapter of *A Portrait* is based on two incidents in Stephen's experience at school. In the first, he is the victim of bullying by a bigger boy called Wells, who pushed him into a ditch of cold, slimy water during recreation. As a result, he develops a fever so that, two mornings afterwards, he has to be taken to the infirmary. It is impossible to say whether such an incident actually took place or, if it did, whether Joyce himself was involved. Ellmann thinks that it is probably a real incident and that it occurred 'probably in the spring of 1891'.[145] This opinion is presumably based on the fact that Joyce received medical attention at some time between February and June of that year, and this is the only occasion in three years when such attention is mentioned in the *Ledger*.[146] By then, of course, Charles Wells had left Clongowes. But Joyce may have altered the facts slightly to preclude unwelcome accusations or complaints – or even to settle old scores! It is certainly not difficult to imagine an incident of this kind in the Clongowes of Joyce's time. The *Punishment Book* refers to a number of Third Line boys (including his classmates Roche and Arthur O'Connell) being quite severely punished in February 1889 for 'throwing boys into snow'.[147] One of the culprits on this occasion, a boy from Rudiments, had been in trouble the previous term for 'shoving a boy into bath'.[148]

The procedure followed by Stephen's prefect, according to which Fr Minister's permission was needed before the boy could go to the infirmary, corresponds exactly to what the 'Rules' prescribed in the matter.[149] The prefect's check that 'he was not foxing' (262), apart from being an obvious precaution in a boarding school, also apparently echoes a phrase used by the prefect of studies, Fr Daly, on such occasions.[150] Once in the infirmary, Joyce would have been familiar both with the place and its custodian, Bro. John Hanly. This is where he had spent his first days in Clongowes. Bro. Michael, as the infirmarian is called in *A Portrait*, is favourably depicted and the verdict of Stephen's fellow-patient Athy, that Bro. Michael was 'very decent' (265), is evidently endorsed.[151] Stephen's impression of Bro. Michael's 'different kind of look' (263) is explained by the fact that Jesuit brothers at the time did not wear clerical collars like the priests and scholastics and dressed, more or less, as laymen.[152] Stephen is puzzled that he has been given no medicine: 'They said you got stinking stuff to drink when you were in the infirmary' (267). Bro. Hanly's remedies were a standing joke among the boys in Clongowes, where he had been since 1881. One of the early issues of *The Rhetorician*, in April 1888, had carried an advertisement for one of these remedies, apparently designed to counteract the ill-effects of Clongowes food:

Hanly's Porter – An Infaillible [*sic*] Remedy for All Complaints and Disorders resulting from the Consumption [*sic*] of Mound-Stiff

A room in the infirmary at Clongowes, about 1900.

Dick-Balls-Slates etc. etc. etc. . . . . 'Salus infirmorum'. . . . . 'Never fails to act'. Sold at Hanly's surgery Clongowes, and of all chemists. Hanly's Porter. To guard against deception as spurious imitations are everywhere being sold, purchasers should assure themselves that cork and bottle bear our Trade Mark 'Celeritas'.[153]

In *A Portrait,* however, Bro. Michael has a function which transcends his medical responsibilities: he is a kind of premonitory image of Parnell.[154]

The Parnell crisis occurred while Joyce was in Clongowes. It is clearly an obsessive topic of conversation in the Dedalus household, but in the school only Athy and Bro. Michael are known to speak of it. In real life, the issue was anything but remote from the boys or the community in Clongowes.

The shadow of Parnell hovered over Joyce's very class from the beginning. On 17 September 1888, shortly after he had come to Clongowes, a Commission of Inquiry had begun to investigate the allegations made by a man called Richard Pigott against Parnell.[155] These had been published in *The Times* the previous year, beginning on 18 April. Two months before the first article appeared, in February 1887, Pigott's sons Joseph and Francis had been enrolled as pupils in Clongowes.[156] In the academic year 1888–89, Joseph was in Rudiments and Francis, with Joyce, in Elements.[157] On 20 February 1889, Pigott was unmasked as a forger and nine days later, on 1 March, in Madrid, he committed suicide. Ellmann, relying on Eoin O'Mahony, says that 'the Jesuit masters went into each classroom to tell the boys not to reveal the news to the sons. One boy did, however, in a terrible scene.'[158] The brothers were not withdrawn from school until the summer and Francis Pigott appears in the Elements photograph, taken in May, sitting in a stiff posture, tight-faced.[159]

Parnell was cited in the O'Shea divorce petition just before Christmas 1889, but the divorce was not granted until 17 November 1890. In Clongowes 'divorces and other indelicate subjects' were spoken of by the 'young men' in the community (meaning the scholastics) 'and others'.[160] Some of their colleagues disapproved and complained to the provincial. The scholastics, it appeared, were also too much given to reading the *Pall Mall Gazette,*[161] which, as Professor Lyons writes, 'was hottest on Parnell's trail' in the period leading to his downfall.[162] The Irish Party split on 6 December, and the Kilkenny by-election which followed soon after provided 'the first trial of strength between the two sides'.[163] As temperatures rose on all sides, the Jesuit provincial Fr Kenny wrote to Fr Conmee in Clongowes on 15 December: 'I saw a fierce letter from a dignitary in Kilkenny saying the greatest enemy the cause of the Church had there at this crisis was Hackett "who had four sons at CWC for nothing". I know this is false.'[164] It was true.[165] 'Hackett' was Dr J. Byrne Hackett of 20 Patrick St, Kilkenny, and sometime coroner in the city. Four of his sons were in Clongowes at the time and eventually six in all were educated there.[166] One of these, Edmund Byrne Hackett, was later involved in Harriet Shaw Weaver's efforts to have *A Portrait* published in America.[167] Another brother, William, became a Jesuit and later edited *The Clongownian*.[168]

If the Hacketts were Parnellites (which, given the way the parties divided in 1890, is what the provincial's letter meant), they were not the only ones to come out of Clongowes in those years. The Rhetoric class of 1888 had resurrected the magazine they had produced in Clongowes, under the original editor Louis Forrest, now a student in Dublin. In the issue for 13 February 1891, he wrote the following fiercely anti-clerical piece:

### Wanted – A Leader

Without delay for the Irish Nation. Must be ubiquitous and omniscient – a Bishops' lickspittle preferred. Need not necessarily be a statesman but must be a rigid exponent of all Christian virtues. He shall have no mind of his own. He shall once a fortnight impart to all his subordinates his political intentions. Once a month he shall in the newspapers make a public profession and confession of all his private actions.

He shall once a year attend in Smithfield Market in the city of Dublin where he shall wash the feet of the there assembled august, venerable, sanctified, eminent, worshipful, members of the Irish Hierarchy. He shall permit himself to be dug in the ribs by every little puny pettifogging country curate; while in his demeanour towards Vicar Generals and Monsignors he shall be expected to insinuate volumes of unspeakable servility. He shall run off messages for Mr Gladstone and to any Englishman who ever said anything friendly of Ireland he must betray an overwhelming sense of gratitude. When he gets from the country a mandate for a certain course of action, he must be prepared at once to discriminate whether he is to obey it, or whether a directly opposite meaning is intended to be conveyed. In relation to political secrets above mentioned he shall be at once liable to blame for divulgence and for silence.

For the performance of these and other similar duties he shall be remunerated in proportion to the money he obtains for the country – say of £40,000 in $4\frac{1}{2}$ millions or something equally microscopic: but a condition of his acceptance shall be that it may at any future time be thrown in his teeth as an evidence of a desire of lucre etc. etc.

For further particulars apply the Archbishop's House or of any streetsweeper.

The tone is remarkably reminiscent of the sentiments of Simon Dedalus and Mr Casey in the Christmas dinner scene in *A Portrait*. Forrest and his friends, to whom *The Rhetorician* circulated, had of course left Clongowes some years when their magazine expressed these bitter thoughts. But they would doubtless have found an echo among quite a number of the boys still in the college, and not in James Joyce alone.

While he is lying in his bed in the infirmary, Stephen wonders if he will die: 'Then he would have a dead mass in the chapel like the way the fellows had told him it was when Little had died' (264). This implied that Little's death had taken place before Stephen was in Clongowes. His imagination of what a funeral would be like is therefore surprisingly circumstantial:

All the fellows would be at the mass, dressed in black, all with sad faces . . . The rector would be there in a cope of black and gold and there would be tall yellow candles on the altar and round the catafalque. And they would carry the coffin out of the chapel slowly and he would be buried in the little graveyard of the community off the main avenue of limes (264–65).

This is, of course, not imagination but a description of something which Joyce had seen in Clongowes. Little died when Joyce was in his second year and, instead of being taken home, was buried in the Jesuit cemetery.[169] According to a tradition in the family, he got a severe drenching while out on a paper-chase 'on the windswept spaces of the Bog of Allen', contracted rheumatic fever and died within five days.[170] The *Journal* of the Higher Line Prefect does not refer to the paper-chase or mention any preceding illness:

December 10th 1890, Wednesday: As usual. Peter Stanislaus Little died in the Infirmary at 1.40 a.m. this morning R.I.P. Boys not permitted to visit the remains.
11th, Thursday: As usual.
12th, Friday: Call 7.30, then as usual till: 10.30 Recreation; 11 Requiem Mass & Funeral; 2.30 Dinner; 7.30 Supper. No studies after supper. All boys wore dress clothes at Mass and Funeral.[171]

The idea of death was frequently enough before the boys in Clongowes, as no doubt it was in most Victorian schools. The prayers of the 'Bona Mors Confraternity' (for a happy death) were recited at benediction, on the first Sunday of the month. And on the feast of All Souls (2 November), when all the faithful departed are prayed for, Fr

Peter Stanislaus Little, who died in December 1890, while Joyce was in Clongowes (from Second of Grammar class photograph, 1888–89).

'The little graveyard of the community off the main avenue of limes' at Clongowes. Little's grave is the first on the left in the top row of crosses, with a stone surround.

Conmee solemnised the occasion by celebrating the boys' Mass himself and saying a few words of explanation beforehand. On that day the altar was draped in black and Stephen's 'yellow candles' were put on it.[172] But, however often death may have been mentioned, nothing could have brought its reality home to them more impressively than the death of one of their own companions. Stan Little was only sixteen when he died. It is not hard to imagine the impact of such a terrible event on the mind of a very small boy. The image of the funeral tends to recur in Stephen's mind, even later on, when he thinks of Clongowes.[173]

The second incident on which the Clongowes chapter is based, following the Christmas dinner episode, involves a whole series of events in the school, stretching over a couple of days at least. It is late March or early April.[174] 'A fellow out of second of grammar', who is a devotee of the new cycling craze in Clongowes, bumps into Stephen while coming out of 'the bicycle house' (303) on his machine. The bicycle house was a shed which had been recently erected just beyond the infirmary.[175] Stephen 'had been thrown lightly on the cinderpath and his spectacles had been broken in three pieces and some of the grit of the cinders had gone into his mouth' (284). The doctor, presumably the one who had first prescribed glasses, had told him not to read without them. The morning after the accident on the cinderpath he writes home for a new pair. Fr Arnall, evidently in his capacity as class-master, gives him permission not to study in the meantime. But during Fr Arnall's Latin class that afternoon, Elements receives a visit from Fr Dolan, the prefect of studies. Having punished Fleming severely for his deficiencies in Latin, the prefect of

Cyclists at Clongowes, about 1888. The photograph was taken by Dominic Kelly, whose caption in Irish is on the back of the original print.

Mr William Gleeson and members of the matriculation class at Clongowes, 1888–89.

studies is about to leave when he happens to notice that Stephen is not writing like the rest. The small boy is too frightened to explain and Fr Dolan disregards the master's explanation on his behalf. Stephen is pandied twice, as a 'lazy little schemer' (294).

The punishment is doubly unjust. Quite apart from the legitimacy of Stephen's excuse, it appears that the prefect of studies' visit to the class is a reaction to events in the Higher Line. He has been into other classes already that morning. Trouble among the older boys has led to a general clampdown and, as Fleming had protested prophetically at lunchtime in the playground, 'we are all to be punished for what other fellows did' (287). What had 'other fellows' done? They had run away to somewhere near the Hill of Lyons and Mr Gleeson and the minister had pursued them on a car. This much remained undisputed amid the welter of rumours about the affair in the Third Line. There was no agreement about why the boys in question had run away. It was because 'Kickham's brother' had 'fecked cash out of the rector's room' (283) and then he and others had shared it out, said Cecil Thunder. No, it was because they had got into the sacristy and drunk the altar wine, according to Wells – and they had been found out by the smell on their breath. But Athy had a third explanation:

they had been caught with two boys from the Third Line one night 'in the square . . . smugging' (285–86). In this version, the name of one of the culprits is Corrigan – a pseudonym, like the names of the two younger boys allegedly involved. The name Thunder had mentioned, Kickham's brother, is evidently no more accurate than the rest of his story. Which of the three versions is correct? The first immediately fades from view and Stephen's subsequent musings concern the other two. The final question concerns what is to happen to those involved. According to Athy, once more, the Third Line boys 'are going to be flogged and the fellows in the higher line got their choice of flogging or being expelled'. In the light of this option, he reports, 'all are taking expulsion except Corrigan. He's going to be flogged by Mr Gleeson' (288).

Can some such incident as the one referred to here be verified in the experience of James Joyce at Clongowes? Some trouble among the senior boys is recorded at the beginning of March 1890. Fr Fegan, who was minister at the time, wrote as follows in his *Journal*:

> 1st, Saturday: As usual till after dinner, when a large number of boys of the Higher and Lower Lines scampered off as if after a hunt. There was no hunt – the escapade had been planned. They all marched home in a body, and came in by playground door. Two or three members of the Community had been sent after them. They arrived back about 6.45. The Higher Line Prefect had been clearing out the Galleries when those outside ran.

Fr James Redmond, the Higher Line Prefect, also recorded the affair, but more summarily. However, he supplies the details that the number involved was sixty-two (almost a third of the total in the two lines) and that they had run off 'to the woods'.[176] It seems quite probable that this incident is at the basis of the narrative in *A Portrait*. The conviction is strengthened by reading Fr Fegan's account of the consequences:

> 3rd, Monday: The boys who joined the run-away on Saturday were punished today. During Night Studies 24 boys were flogged; the rest are to get ferulae tomorrow. Three boys refused to allow themselves to be flogged but after a while 2 of them agreed to it. The boy who persisted in refusal was told it would necessarily mean his leaving the house – so he ran away along with two others at about 7 o'c.
>
> 4th, Tuesday: A boy who had been in the row and who had been giving trouble for some time before was called at 6.30 and expelled. Sent to town by the 8 o'c train that he might not meet the boys anywhere. His things had been packed the evening before.

Fr Redmond adds: 'Boys told by Fr Minister that they were not to leave the playground to follow hunts etc. without leave'.

Such an incident would naturally have given rise to the most lively speculation among the boys. But their version (or rather versions) of the facts could have borne only the vaguest resemblance to the account Fr Fegan was in a position to give. About the 'run-away' itself they could hardly not have known, in view of the numbers who had taken part in it. The punishments which followed would also have been public knowledge in a general way – although, of course, the Third Line would not have been in the big study from which the twenty-four destined for a flogging were either conspicuously absent or else publicly summoned on the Monday evening. The other circumstances – some refusing and then agreeing to be flogged, one running away all over again and another being expelled – could only have been the subject of the most uncertain rumour. Finally, Fr Fegan's warning about not leaving the playground without permission, if addressed to all the boys, would have deepened the mystery still further for those who had not been involved.

As it actually occurred, this incident lacks the more sinister note introduced by the mention of 'smugging' and some kind of illicit contact between older and younger boys in the square.[176a] Nothing of the kind appears to have been involved on this occasion. But, in the very segregated world of Clongowes in those times, it would be unrealistic to imagine that such things never occurred. The system of lines was, in part, designed to prevent them happening and behaviour in the square was subject to particularly strict regulation: 'All are to understand that Silence and Propriety are to be observed in the Square. All unnecessary delay, conversation, and games of every description are forbidden in the square'. Transgressions were severely dealt with when they occurred. They seem to have been very infrequent.[177] In Joyce's time one boy (in First of Grammar) was flogged for 'smoking in the Square' and two others were severely pandied for 'talking' in the same place.[178] One was from the Lower Line and one from the Third Line but they were actually members of the same class (Third of Grammar)[179] and their conversation may well have been utterly harmless. But the law was strictly applied in such matters. Four years before Joyce's arrival in Clongowes, unwelcome attentions had been paid to some younger boys by a number of their seniors on a couple of occasions and this led to consequences very similar to those described by Fr Fegan in the case already referred to.[180] Such a scandal might have remained a topic of surreptitious gossip in after years and Joyce may have heard about it. As we have seen in the case of Little's death, he was quite capable of relegating events he had experienced himself to the period before

Fr James Daly ('Fr Dolan'): close-up from photograph of the Clongowes community, 1887–88.

Stephen Dedalus came to Clongowes, so that Stephen merely hears about them. For his own purposes, he could just as easily describe events about which he himself had merely heard as if they had happened in Stephen's time.

Whatever the truth may be about events in the Higher Line, Joyce himself assured Herbert Gorman that he had been pandied by the prefect of studies, as he describes in *A Portrait*.[181] This part of the novel helped to make Fr James Daly, easily recognised under his pseudonym of Dolan, famous. But long before the book appeared, Fr Daly was well on the way to becoming a legend in Clongowes. By 1916, when it was published, he had been prefect of studies there continuously for just short of thirty years. A Galway man, he had been educated in the Jesuit college in Namur and, for one year, in Tullabeg.[182] After his training as a Jesuit and some other teaching assignments, he came to Clongowes in 1887, just one year ahead of Joyce. He was then forty-one. The appointment seems to have been part of a campaign to make the amalgamation work and to ensure that the combined colleges of Tullabeg and Clongowes did not fall below the standard already reached by Tullabeg on its own. He had shown his capacity for the job during a brief spell as prefect of studies in Limerick. During his two years there, 'the profession of idling was at an end among the boys'.[183] He quickly set himself to end it in Clongowes too.

His impact was immediate. Traditional breaks from study, like the expedition to the Punchestown races, were ended. *The Rhetorician*, pursuing a tenuous underground existence, muttered darkly that it was 'for many a bucket of cold water thrown on their ardour in the preparation just now at its height for the ensuing examinations'.[184] But the threat implied was not carried out and the first of a long series of excellent Intermediate results under Fr Daly was duly obtained in the summer.[185] By 1890 the editors of *The Rhetorician* were past pupils. But even with two years' distance between them, they could not get him out of their systems and there were numerous references to his 'eagle spectacles in the study' and his dismaying enthusiasm for work.[186]

Fr Dolan is seen only once in *A Portrait* and then briefly. Yet Joyce manages to convey both Fr James Daly's appearance and the impact he made on classes as he moved about the school. The prefect of studies in the novel arrives suddenly, unexpected although we have already heard that he is on the move. He carries on a pretence of questioning Fr Arnall about 'any lazy idle little loafers that want flogging' in his class, while in reality catechising the boys in a loud voice about the necessity of work (293). When two suitable victims fall under his eye, he punishes them summarily by way of warning and departs, vowing that he will return every day. In particular, we are left with the image of his 'whitegrey not young face, his baldy whitegrey head with fluff at the sides of it, the steel rims of his spectacles and his nocoloured eyes looking through the glasses' (295).[187]

As usual Joyce's memory – in his case based on quite a short acquaintance with Fr Daly – is corroborated by others who knew him longer and better. Fr Laurence Kieran, who came to Clongowes as a boy in 1893 and later succeeded Fr Daly as prefect of studies, recalled his first sighting:

> Class had not been long in progress when a heavy step was heard on the corridor, in a moment the door was flung open and Fr Daly burst into the room. His appearance filled me with apprehension. As he stood before the class he seemed the very embodiment of strength, energy and determination. Though not then as stout as he afterwards became, he looked decidedly big and, as he paced up and down, puffing, expanding his chest and issuing instructions, he decidedly left one under the impression that it would be more prudent to carry them out. His hair, which he wore very tightly cropped, was then turning grey; a beard showed over his Roman collar and gave him a weird appearance; but it was the penetrating and uneasy glance of his small grey eyes which most of all inspired fear in those meeting him for the first time. . . .[188]

Fr Daly: photograph taken in 1914. Joyce's description of the prefect of studies in *A Portrait* fits Fr Daly in old age much better than the Fr Daly he would actually have known.

Another recollection of Fr Daly described the speeches with which he regaled the slacker and how the speech was 'punctuated, driven home, by loud-resounding strokes of the pandybat, not administered one after another quickly, but at regular intervals'.[189] Fr Kieran insisted that 'beneath that awe-inspiring exterior there beat a most kindly and sympathetic heart' and that 'his voice . . . raised every day in expostulation and warning and encouragement' and 'his old clumsy pandybat . . . seen and heard and felt at frequent intervals' did not in fact terrorise the boys or make them unhappy. Indeed, he concluded, 'no word he spoke in rebuke, not even his pandybat, caused a pang which endured for more than five minutes.'[190]

Stephen Dedalus would not have agreed. But even Stephen reflected afterwards, when coming to the end of his schooldays, that during all his years in Clongowes and Belvedere 'he had received only two pandies and, though these had been dealt him in the wrong, he knew that he had often escaped punishment' (415–16). The system in

The stairs to the right of the refectory door at Clongowes and the door into Serpentine corridor which leads to the Castle.

'The low dark narrow corridor' to the Castle, about 1910. Joyce thought he remembered 'portraits of the saints and great men of the order' in this corridor. Those in the photograph are of distinguished past pupils. His own portrait is now among them.

Clongowes was harsh enough in Joyce's time. Dominic Kelly wrote an article on 'The ethics of corporal punishment' in *The Rhetorician* in 1889, in which he deplored the continuing 'torture of the whistling cane and resounding pandybat' and 'the constant, unnatural dread, unworthy of a human being, of being beaten like a dog for the most trivial offence'. These he described as 'the ordinary daily sights and sounds around us'. [191] But Fr James Daly seems to have been eccentric rather than sadistic. [192] And Clongowes bears no comparison in this matter with the cruelty reported by other contemporary writers of their public schools in England. [193]

According to the *Punishment Book,* James Joyce (unlike Stephen Dedalus) was pandied on three occasions. Two of these have been mentioned already. The other was on 7 February 1889, shortly after he turned seven. He, Gerald Gill and Arthur McKenna were sent out by Fr Power (teaching them Latin at the time?), for 'forgetting to bring book to class'. This is the first occasion on which Joyce is mentioned in the records as having been punished; it happened in relation to Fr Power's class; and the number of pandies was two. These three facts recall the incident in the novel. But it cannot, of course, be the same incident. The *Punishment Book* contained only the names of those who were 'sent out', not those who received summary punishment in the course of Fr Daly's travels around the classes. And when 'sent out' in this way, boys would have gone to one of the prefects to be punished, not to Fr Daly. [194] Of Joyce's punishment at his hands, there is no record except his own. [195]

Nor is there any record of Stephen Dedalus' famous reaction to the only instance of being pandied that Joyce allows him to remember. The 'Rules' stipulated that 'the time appointed for seeing the Rector is during the play-hours after breakfast and lunch. Except at these times, he should not be disturbed except on urgent business'. Stephen's business is urgent. Fleming had urged him to 'go straight up to the rector and tell him about it after dinner' (298). But the rector is a remote and awesome figure, met with parents on arrival and after that only glimpsed occasionally, performing his priestly functions on special occasions like the morning of his first holy communion in the chapel or the procession to the woods on the feast of the Sacred Heart in June. It would not be the first time he had been to the rector: once before 'he had been called to the castle' (248). But the circumstances made this visit a much more daunting prospect. He is in an agony of indecision as he leaves the refectory: 'if he went on with the fellows he could never go up to the rector because he could not leave the playground for that' (300). The 'Rules' stated that 'No one may leave the place appointed for Recreation without the Prefect's permission, and those who arrive late must say why they were delayed'. At the last moment, Stephen turns up the stairs. The door into the Serpentine corridor, connecting the school with the Castle, opened off the first landing. Joyce's description of the topography of Stephen's memorable journey (301–02) is exact, save in one detail. There were in fact no 'little doors' on 'the narrow dark corridor'. The 'rooms of the community' were in the Castle, on the second floor. At no stage would Stephen have passed them. Joyce may have confused them with a number of doors opening off a passageway in the Castle itself, just beyond the Serpentine. It is one of his very few errors of this kind. There may well have been portraits of Jesuit saints and 'great men of the order' on the walls of the corridor in Joyce's time. The portrait of Fr Peter Kenny, the founder of Clongowes, whom he describes precisely as 'wrapped in a big cloak', is still to be seen close by in the round room of the Castle. But the others are gone now, having made way since the start of the present century for portraits of distinguished past Clongownians. In the present year Joyce himself has at last found a place on the corridor he has made famous.

The rector of Clongowes for practically all of Joyce's time was Fr John Conmee. He had been at school there himself in the sixties and knew it well.[196] He came back as prefect of studies in 1883 and became rector as well two years later. In 1887, Fr Daly relieved him of his original office and left him free to cope with the heavy responsibilities he had inherited as a result of the amalgamation with Tullabeg the previous year. During his remaining years as rector, the college was never free of extreme financial anxieties. The provincial, and even the general in Rome, worried about Clongowes' heavy debts. But their regard for its rector never wavered.[197] After finishing his term as rector of Clongowes Fr Conmee was appointed to a succession of responsible jobs: prefect of studies in Belvedere (1891–92), prefect of studies in UCD (1893–95), superior of St Francis Xavier's Church in Gardiner St (1897–1905), provincial (1905–09) and finally, just before his death, rector of Milltown Park (1909–10). For nine of these years, he also acted as consultor to other provincials.

But despite this series of high administrative positions, he never became distant from those around him. Few men have been so warmly regarded by everyone who knew him, superiors, colleagues and pupils alike.[198] Michael Egan, an older contemporary of Joyce in Clongowes, wrote of Fr Conmee as 'a prince among men, all kindliness and courtesy and with an exquisite literary gift that made his conversation a delight even to schoolboys'.[199] Another of his former pupils, who had been at school from 1882 to 1888, described what he was like:

One of the portraits Joyce did see in Clongowes: 'Father Peter Kenny sitting in a chair wrapped in a big cloak'. This portrait is now in the round room of the Castle.

In appearance refined and debonair, in manner always genial, in stature more than medium, his features rounded rather than aquiline, his presence invariably produced the impression of an active mind and a personality not only at ease with its environment, but ever alert and responsive to whatever 'time and the hour' was capable of.[200]

The notion of Fr Conmee as the classical Victorian Jesuit, refined and 'West British' in manner, is mistaken: 'His accent was charged with a Connaught "burr" which added homeliness to his utterance'.[201] He was austere: the skull Stephen Dedalus saw on the rector's desk is undoubtedly an authentic memory (whatever symbolic overtones it may otherwise possess): 'With Fr Conmee there was without doubt that certain austerity which engendered a feeling of discipline because it seemed to emanate from a personal discipline of his own.'[202] But this did not mask or suppress his humanity (as it perhaps did in Fr William Henry, Joyce's rector and prefect of studies later on in Belvedere). As Con Little remembered, 'it was an austerity tempered by a generous outlook, a gentle and humorous affability, a wholehearted and complete understanding and an indulgent appreciation of the stuff and nature of youth.'[203] The skull on the desk was far from being the whole story. There is a touch of amiable eccentricity about the Turkish smoking-hat in which Fr Conmee received visitors in Gardiner St when he was provincial,[204] and the Pomeranian dog he took with him when he went on visitation of the houses in his province.[205] In Clongowes, despite his lack of athletic skill or even of much understanding of games,[206] he was universally popular with the boys. He himself was never happier than

> in the midst of a throng of clamorous Third-liners. For them he had as many jokes and stories and elusive ways of drawing out funds of spirited repartee, as with the elders. Old and young knew perfectly well that there was no better appreciator of their capabilities howsoever displayed – be it in a joke, a song, a concert, or a play or in an achievement of scholarship or debate, than was their rector.[207]

James Joyce felt the same as everyone else about Fr Conmee: in *A Portrait* (and later in *Ulysses*), he added his own tribute.

The author of *Old Times in the Barony* is appropriately first glimpsed in the novel, by reader and diminutive schoolboy alike, 'sitting at a desk writing'. In the interview which follows, he is everything that Fr Dolan had not been in the parallel scene in Fr Arnall's classroom. There is a skull on the desk and the room is 'solemn', but the rector has a 'kindlooking face' (302). When Stephen hesitates, terrified at his own audacity in coming to the rector, Fr Conmee waits encouragingly. Unlike Fr Dolan, who had had to ask it twice, Fr Conmee knows Stephen's name without being told. He questions him patiently and follows his stumbling, tearful narrative until everything is clear and the small boy is satisfied. As Stephen withdraws, 'Don John Conmee' bows courteously to him and Stephen returns the bow.[208]

Stephen's excited return to the playground is described with Joyce's usual care. When he has come back along 'the low dark narrow corridor' and 'down the staircase' to the refectory door, he hurries 'through the two corridors and out into the air' (304). The first of these 'two corridors' was the short gallery, where the Third Line playrooms were. A door to the playground opened off the east side of this gallery, opposite the playrooms. But this door was for the Higher Line and Lower Line boys only, and Stephen does not use it. Instead he goes through the short gallery and along the bottom corridor of the Carbery Building (virtually a continuation of the short gallery, beyond the junction with the long gallery). The door for the Third Line was past the swimming-bath and just short of the entrance to the infirmary. From there Stephen can hear 'the cries of the fellows on the playgrounds'. But he has to run 'across the cinder-path'[209] and back past the outside of the Carbery Building and the study hall to reach his companions over on 'the third line playground' behind the Castle (304). Once there, he imparts his news in a scene reminiscent of Paddy Rath's triumph after the famous Phoenix cricket match of 1891.[210]

The chapter ends with the fellows' exultant cheers for 'the decentest rector that was ever in Clongowes' (305) still echoing. But there is a distancing effect created by the absence of any individual names in this final episode. 'The fellows' have already begun to fade into anonymity, Clongowes recedes into the past and the first phase of Stephen's schooldays is coming to an end.

Joyce himself does not seem to have left Clongowes at the end of the summer term, as A Portrait clearly depicts Stephen doing. A superficial review of the records in Clongowes gives the impression that his parents followed the strong recommendation of the Prospectus, which asked that boys be withdrawn only at the summer vacation.[211] In the first place the half-yearly account sent out on 1 September 1891 to cover the winter term was never paid.[212] In the second place, Joyce's name, although entered in the Register for Rudiments, has been subsequently cancelled. This would suggest that he did not actually return in September at all; the account was sent out and the entry made in anticipation of an event which never

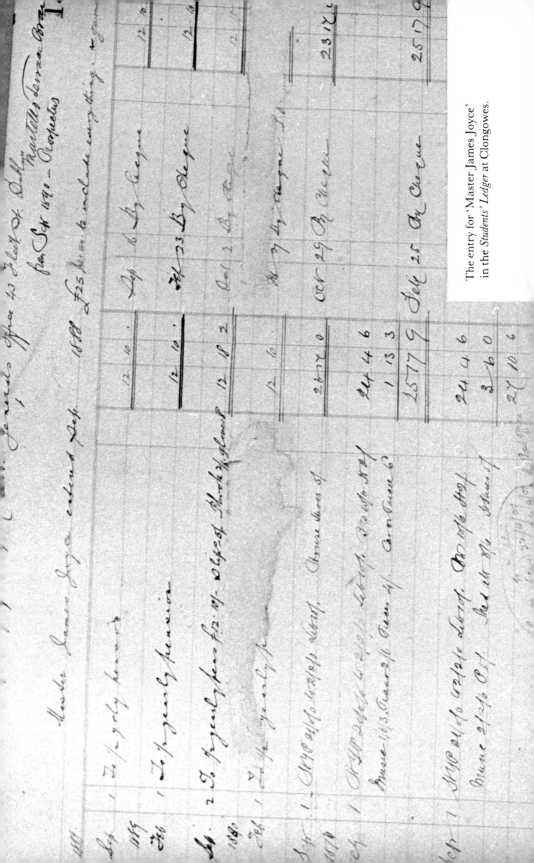

The entry for 'Master James Joyce'
in the *Students' Ledger* at Clongowes.

took place. But a closer look shows that this is a mistake. At the very least, it can be said that the Joyces gave no indication of their intention to remove their son. Otherwise the account sent out would not have included the half-yearly pension for the coming term.[213] It was not, of course, John Joyce's way to plan very far ahead. It could be surmised that events had caught up with him suddenly, so that James's removal from Clongowes happened abruptly. But the register of classes, which contains his name, would not have been made out for some weeks at least, until all the boys were back and classes had somewhat stabilised. Thus the 1889 register of classes was only made out in November.[214] This seems to indicate that Joyce actually came back for some weeks at least, and possibly longer, possibly for the whole winter term.

In the light of a final consideration, it seems quite probable that he did spend the full term and was only withdrawn at Christmas. According to Ellmann, the family was still at Martello Terrace on 26 October 1891, when Eva was born.[215] He puts the move to Blackrock as 'at the beginning of 1892'.[216] In the Clongowes *Register,* where Joyce's name appears for Rudiments and is then cancelled, his address is given as Leoville House, Blackrock.[217] The Joyces had evidently already moved, or at least expected to move shortly and knew their future address, by the time the *Register* in Clongowes was filled in. Perhaps the move took place a little earlier than Ellmann suggests. But it seems quite certain in the light of the *Register's* evidence that Joyce returned to Clongowes for several months in the winter of 1891.

When he was finally withdrawn, the reason was presumably related to his father's inability to pay the fees any longer. The usual fee in Clongowes was forty guineas a year, payable in half-yearly instalments, with certain automatic additions and other extras which were optional.[218] James Joyce was accepted on special terms in 1888: '£25 per an[num] to include everything'. John Joyce's cheques for £12-10-0 were paid within a few weeks of receiving the account in September and February. In 1889 the same pension was charged, with a few small items added, retrospective to the preceding half-year: a prayer-book and gloves, both probably in connection with his first holy communion, and the slippers or house-shoes on which the 'Rules' insisted. Payment was a little less prompt, but not unduly so. For 1890 the terms were altered and the full forty guineas was charged. Supplements for 'washing, mending etc.' and for 'library, games, amusements' were automatically added. Joyce was also now charged for the first time for schoolbooks and for getting his hair cut. He began to take piano lessons, which meant further additions to the account. On one occasion the doctor had been called, which was another eight and sixpence on the bill. And he had to be kept in house-shoes. The cost of his son's education was rising at a time when John Joyce's economic position was in decline.[219] The September 1890 account was not settled for almost two months. The account submitted a year later, for almost thirty pounds, was never settled. After that, no more accounts were sent.

Was finance the reason for Joyce's withdrawal? It is noteworthy that the Bursar made no effort to pursue payment of the account.[220] Nor did he formally write off the loss and mark the account closed, as he usually did in cases where payment was not sought. This was very far from being the only bill unpaid and it was certainly not the largest. Apart from accounts not settled, there was also quite a number of pupils who had been received free. Could Joyce not have been kept on by some alteration of the terms, perhaps by some of the 'wangling with influential personalities' by his father, such as Gorman imagines went on later to get James and his brothers into Belvedere for nothing?[221]

Fr Conmee's replacement as rector in June 1891 by Fr Matthew Devitt may have influenced the situation. It was easier for the provincial, Fr Kenny, to bring the full weight of his anxieties about Clongowes' financial state to bear on a new rector. Fr Conmee had already been in office three years when Fr Kenny was made provincial in 1888. 'I assure you I am alarmed about C.W.C.', he wrote to Fr Devitt in September 1891,[222] '. . . the extraordinary debt on the house and the absolute necessity for economy and saving make your case quite exceptional. I am absolutely certain it is in your power to save C.W.C. but this can't be done if you don't look after little things.' The idea of Clongowes 'refusing to pay its lawful debts' was intolerable. 'You can easily save a £1000 this year if you look after the sixpences'. The provincial went on to stipulate such details as how many out-matches in cricket (four) and football (three), each of which entailed entertainment of visiting teams, Clongowes was to undertake in the coming year. In due course he would put before Fr Devitt 'several other things that I was asked to see after last visitation but were kept back by me till now in view of the change of rectors'. He probably should have insisted earlier (i.e. with Fr Conmee) 'on a different policy being pursued', but 'not wishing to give pain without hope of good coming from it, I let things take their course.'

A month later Fr Kenny raised a different, but not unrelated, matter – the finances of Belvedere, where Fr Devitt had been rector before coming to Clongowes: 'How many boys do you think you had last year at Belvedere? How many not paying?'[223] But, despite all the financial stringency, that is the nearest the provincial comes in the letters which are extant to the question of fees. In his very long letter

An almost certainly authentic signature by Joyce, the earliest extant, discovered in a book from the Third Line library at Clongowes, *The Life of the holy Patriarch S. Ignatius of Loyola, Author, and Founder of the Society of Jesus*, published in 1622. Such defacing of library books was contrary to the school rules, but there is no record of Joyce having been punished for his transgression on this occasion.

of 21 September, he proposes, among other things, that 'much might be done in reducing your guests' bills' and explains that 'by guests I mean those who come to see their boys'. But he never suggests anything about pursuing unpaid accounts, sending away those who had not paid, or reducing the number of boys who were being educated on special terms or for no fees at all. It may be that Mr Joyce did not attempt to discuss his position with the new rector who, to the boys at least, 'seemed . . . cold and hard' by comparison with Fr Conmee.[224] If there had been any kind of special understanding with the latter, as a friend or even a relation of the family, John Stanislaus may have felt there was no future for his son in Clongowes once his own finances had dwindled and Fr Conmee was gone. But this is mere speculation: we do not really know.

Kevin Sullivan wondered if 'a recurrence of the illness he suffered during the spring' might not have contributed to the decision to withdraw Joyce later in the year.[225] There is no evidence for this. According to Stanislaus, he was 'always in good health'[226] and the *Ledger* supports this. Nor, unlike Stephen Dedalus, was Joyce unhappy in Clongowes. Stanislaus, who was taken to see his brother in school on a few occasions, remembered him as 'perfectly free of his surroundings, a boy amongst boys'.[227] Stanislaus would have been so young at the time that the accuracy of his recollection might be doubted. But Dominick O'Connor, who came to Clongowes in 1891 at the age of thirteen, had said the same some years before Stanislaus' memoir appeared. He recalled Joyce as 'by no means a melancholy, frightened child (as he is sometimes portrayed), but as a blithe and happy boy'.[28]

Charles Stewart Parnell died in October 1891 and Christmas that year was marred in the Dedalus household by the memory of his death and the betrayal which had gone before it. It may have been a time of some regret for James Joyce personally, and not just because of his inherited loyalty to Parnell. The Christmas dinner scene was originally placed in chapter two of *A Portrait*,[229] which is where it belongs in the chronology of Joyce's own life, just after he had left Clongowes. A glimpse of his feelings can perhaps be had from the picture he gives of Stephen 'at his table in Bray the morning after the discussion at the Christmas dinner table', nostalgically covering the page of his exercise-book 'with the names and addresses of his classmates' (317) in Clongowes. Stephen is merely at home for the holidays. The scene more accurately reflects the feelings of Joyce himself, who has left Clongowes for good.

# TWO

# Belvedere College 1893–98

An interval of some fifteen months elapsed between the time James Joyce left Clongowes and went to his next Jesuit school, Belvedere College in the centre of Dublin. The family stayed in Blackrock for about a year. Once he got over whatever nostalgia he may have felt for Clongowes, Joyce set to work educating himself while the other children of school-going age were sent to the local convent.[1] It is easy to see how freedom like this at such an early age in a precocious and talented boy like Joyce would lead to a certain contempt for the restraints and limitations of normal schooling later on. At the end of 1892 or early in 1893, the Joyces moved to Dublin and, after a brief stop in lodgings, settled at 14 Fitzgibbon St. It was, as Ellmann remarks, 'the last of their good addresses'.[2] Belvedere was just across Mountjoy Square from this house, but James and Stanislaus were first sent to the Christian Brothers' school around the corner in North Richmond St.[3] This interlude is only hinted at in *A Portrait*: Joyce seems to have shared his parents' prejudice that being educated 'with Paddy Stink and Mickey Mud', as Simon Dedalus put it, was not worthy of him (319). According to Stanislaus, he and James stayed only 'a few months' in North Richmond St, before being transferred to Belvedere.[4] Their names are enrolled in the *Prefect of Studies' Book* for 6 April 1893.

It is generally assumed that the transfer was effected through the good offices of Fr Conmee. He was not, as Simon Dedalus thinks, provincial at the time. Nor was he prefect of studies in Belvedere.[5] After leaving Clongowes in 1891, he had been appointed to this position. But his health, always a cause of anxiety, seems to have necessitated a change after one year.[6] The following year, he remained in the college until the summer in the capacity of teacher and director of the sodality. However, although no longer in charge of studies, Fr Conmee would naturally have wielded considerable influence with his successor, the rector Fr Thomas Wheeler. And, no doubt, he would have been happy to use it in the interest of James Joyce and his brother. It was part of Conmee's charm that he did not forget people.

In addition, Fr Conmee's possible part in the Joyce boys' entrance to Belvedere raises once more the question of whether he was related to them in some way, or was at least a friend of the family. It is noteworthy that, in *Ulysses,* Joyce feels familiar enough with him to

Belvedere College, shown during or some time after the rectorship of Fr Nicholas Tomkin (1900–08)

make us privy, for a few pages, to his inner life. And, in his reported conversation with Mrs Sheehy in Mountjoy Square, one detail may be of significance in the present instance. 'Father Conmee', we hear, 'was wonderfully well indeed. He would go to Buxton probably for the waters' (281). Shortly before James and Stanislaus were admitted to Belvedere, the provincial Fr Kenny wrote to inform the general in Rome that Fr Conmee was seriously unwell and to request permission for him to visit 'the baths', in order to recuperate. In July 1896 and again in July 1897, the provincial (by then Fr Keating) wrote to seek permission for Fr Conmee to go to 'Germany' and 'the continent' respectively, for the sake of his health.[7] Joyce may have heard about Fr Conmee's visits to the baths (Buxton was one of a number mentioned in a letter from the general in 1893)[8] from his friends, Richard and Eugene Sheehy. But, on the other hand, his knowledge of Fr Conmee's health and his movements during the summer may point to more than merely formal acquaintance with the ex-rector of Clongowes on the part of the Joyce family. This may help to explain the hand he apparently took in expediting the next stage of James Joyce's education, if any explanation beyond the boy's obvious ability is required.

Although April may seem a strange time of the year to send boys to a new school for the first time, it constituted no problem whatever. In 1892–93 'new boys' were being admitted to Belvedere all through the year, including two after the Joyces, one on 6 May and one as late as 6 June.[9] Nor was there any pressure on space: quite the contrary.[10] But could John Joyce afford the £5-10-0 per term which was charged for two brothers, to say nothing of £7 or even £9 when Charles and George entered the college (as they both eventually did)?[11] The answer was no and Joyce was, like Stephen Dedalus, 'a free boy' in Belvedere for the whole of his time there (341) and his brothers after him. In the *Cash Book* recording the payment of fees for this period, there is no reference of any kind to payment by John Stanislaus Joyce. There is no room for ambiguity or doubt in this matter. The bursar usually noted the boys' names when entering payments by their parents or guardians; to avoid confusion with names which occurred more often (as Joyce, for example), he would add the address as well.[12] It was in ensuring this exemption from fees that Fr Conmee's influence may well have been sought.

The fact that they paid no fees did not make the Joyces at all unique. The *Cash Book* shows that, of the twenty-eight boys in James Joyce's class in 1893–94, only twenty-one paid fees and, of these, only twelve paid the full amount. Since the records are far from complete, it is quite possible that some of the boys who appear to have paid no fees were no longer in the college, and do not appear in the *Cash Book*

1892-93.

New Boys

| NAME. | BORN. | ENTRANCE. |
|---|---|---|
| Macey Joseph | 8 Nov. 80 | Mar. 7. |
| Storey John Francis | 3 Jun 87 | |
| Fallon Austin | Dec. 83 | Ap. 5 |
| Joyce James Augustine | 2 Feb. 82 | 6 |
| Joyce Stanislaus | 17 Dec 85 | " |
| Waldrick Joseph | 2 Ap. 86 | May 6 |
| Kilcarey Roderick Roy | 10 81 | Jun 6 |

Entry for James and Stanislaus Joyce in the *Prefect of Studies' Book*, on their admission to Belvedere, 6 April 1893.

for this reason. But it is quite clear that, in Belvedere as in Clongowes, it was the practice to educate some boys entirely free of charge, if necessity dictated this, and to give 'special terms' to others. J. F. Byrne, Joyce's friend 'Cranly', for example, paid only £1 per term: within four months of coming to Belvedere (in September 1892), his mother had died, leaving him an orphan.[13] He lived with his middle-aged cousin Miss Mary Fleming in Earl Essex St (they were later to move to a famous address, 7 Eccles St) and it was she who made these reduced payments.[14] Although the boys in Belvedere more or less all came from the emerging Catholic middle class, this term denoted then as now a fairly wide range economically and it is unlikely that James Joyce either felt himself to be or actually was conspicuously underprivileged because his parents were paying no fees for him.

It was the vigorous rectorship of Fr Thomas Finlay, from 1883–88, which brought Belvedere to the stage of physical and academic development in which Joyce found it in 1893. Finlay, remembered in *A Portrait* as 'the squat peasant form of the professor of economics' in UCD in Joyce's time as a student there (456), was one of the most remarkable Jesuits in the Irish province at this period. Having acted as prefect of studies in both Limerick and Tullabeg (under William Delany) while still a scholastic, he was offered a professorship in the Royal University in 1882 and managed to combine the position with his Belvedere rectorship, retaining it (under different titles) until 1930.[15] When he died, ten years later, his obituary spoke of him as 'in a true sense . . . the second founder of Belvedere . . . which he had led out of the stages of childhood to the full growth of manhood and maturity'.[16]

His arrival coincided with the new demands and opportunities provided by the Intermediate Education Act of 1878 as well as the restructuring of the Royal University under Jesuit management. This provided funds with which to pay the interest on a building loan, through the system of payment for results which the Act introduced.[17] It also stimulated interest in Catholic schools to complete the secondary cycle and continue into university, an interest which had been previously lacking.[18] Fr Finlay proceeded to build a new school on the site of the coachhouses at the back of Belvedere House. Between the two there was a small garden, with grass plots, pathways, flowerbeds and, in the centre, a fountain. Prior to this development, all the classes had been conducted in Belvedere House itself. To provide for further expansion, he purchased 5 Great Denmark St (Belvedere House is No. 6), formerly the town residence of Lord Fingall, whose garden he turned into a hall – this acted as a theatre and later also as a gymnasium.[19] The fourth side of the quadrangle formed by Belvedere House, this hall and the new school

*Belvedere College S.J.*
*Great Denmark St Dublin*

ELVEDERE COLLEGE, Great Denmark Street, is conducted by the Fathers of the Society of Jesus. . To parents resident in or near the City of Dublin, who desire to combine in the education of their sons the discipline and teaching of a public school with the very important influences of home life, it offers the advantages of a High Class Grammar School.

The Course of Education comprises the usual Grammar School subjects. In the three Higher Forms boys are prepared for the Intermediate Examinations. Candidates are also prepared for the Entrance Examinations of the College of Surgeons, for Civil Service Examinations, Preliminary Examinations for Solicitors' Apprentices, &c

The School Year is divided into three Terms: First Term, from August till December; Second Term, from December till April; Third Term, from April till July. The Pension for each of these Terms is £3, payable in advance, within the first month of the Term.

Drawing of Belvedere from the 1888 Prospectus, with the front facade (including the low walls on either side of Belvedere House) as Joyce would have known it. Exaggerated perspective makes the 'yard' at the back appear about three times as large as it is.

building was what Joyce calls 'the shed that flanked the garden' (322), a simple arcade which offered the only available shelter in wet weather. This was the complex of buildings which James and Stanislaus Joyce entered in April 1893.

Belvedere House itself is virtually unchanged from the time of Joyce, except that the windows in front 'were filled with small panes of glass, usual in all houses of the period' and, instead of the great iron gates on either side, 'two low walls stretched to the adjoining houses, and in each wall a small door'.[20] The boys entered by the right-hand door[21] and would have come through Belvedere House only on such special occasions as the night of the play or an interview with the rector in the house itself. This was evidently no longer in use for school purposes in Joyce's day, which would explain his otherwise surprising failure to make any mention at all of the magnificent interior decoration in the hall, on the stairs, and in the L-shaped suite of rooms, dedicated to Apollo, Diana and Venus respectively, on the first floor. As soon as he had provided alternative accommodation for the boys, Fr Finlay had done his best to restore these beautiful rooms to their original splendour and elegance.[22] Today this house and the school building (which now has a twin-extension joined to it, as large as itself) are all that remain of Joyce's Belvedere.

Fr Finlay's school building contained a chapel and vestry on a level with the garden, science laboratories and classrooms on the first floor and classrooms on the second floor. The attic above was used to store stage properties.[23] Joyce refers to three different classes – numbers one, two and six. From two remarks by J. F. Byrne it is possible to work out which Joyce's classrooms were from 1894–98. According to Byrne, there were 'four classrooms numbered 1 to 4 respectively for the senior, middle, junior and preparatory grades'.[24] This is exactly the number of classrooms on the top floor of Fr Finlay's building, to which Byrne's description clearly refers. Elsewhere he recalls sharing 'no. 3' with Joyce in 1894–95, Joyce's Junior Grade year, and explains how 'at the west and east walls there were folding doors, opening respectively to the preparatory and middle grade classrooms'.[25] From this it can be deduced that the classes were numbered from one to four, running from right to left (east to west) as you face this building from the yard,[26] and with two windows to each classroom. The actual arrangement of classrooms corresponds to Joyce's text, scrupulously accurate as always in such matters. Stephen is clearly in his next-to-last year (Middle Grade) when he speaks of being 'in number two' (321).[27] He and his classmate Heron are 'virtual heads of the school' because 'the fellows in number one' (Senior Grade) are 'undistinguished dullards' (324). Joyce also refers to the end of Stephen's 'first term in the college when he was in number six' (327). This was presumably a classroom downstairs on the first floor. Sullivan, in *Joyce Among the Jesuits,* liked to imagine Mr Dempsey 'standing by one of the great second-floor windows overlooking Great Denmark Street',[28] on the false premise that Joyce attended classes in Belvedere House. The windows of Joyce's classrooms overlooked the garden. This is why, on one occasion when the rector is delayed on his

The senior school building at Belvedere, referred to as 'the schoolhouse' in *A Portrait*, taken in 1906 from the steps of Belvedere House. The theatre, which also served as an examination hall and gymnasium, is on the left and 'the shed that flanked the garden' on the right. The ground floor of the school building contained the vestry (left) and the chapel. The four 'Grade' classrooms were on the top floor, in ascending seniority from left to right.

way to the religious knowledge class, 'a boy from his post at the window' is able to see him 'come from the house' (359). 'The house' in question is Belvedere House, where Fr Henry and the rest of the Jesuit community lived. The only school-building in Joyce's time which looked out on Great Denmark St was number five, beside Belvedere House. The ground floor was given over to Fr James Cullen's 'Messenger Office'[29] and the floors above to the preparatory school, physically but not yet administratively separate from the rest of the college. Joyce remembered this accurately in *Ulysses* as 'the little house' (*U* 281), the name by which it was then commonly known,[30] But he was never a pupil in it himself.

Sullivan somewhat overstates the social difference between Joyce's two schools when he says that education at Belvedere 'was a necessity for those less fortunate but equally intent on getting ahead in the world so that someday perhaps they might be in a position to send their own sons to schools like Clongowes Wood. To pass from one to the other was to take a perceptible step down the social ladder'.[31] This view is too much coloured by the particular circumstances of Joyce's transfer. There were boys in Clongowes who were in no position to pay any fees at all. There were boys in Belvedere whose parents could easily have afforded the Clongowes fees but chose not to send their sons away from home. Many pupils of one school subsequently became pupils of the other. However, it has to be admitted that the more usual transition was from Belvedere to Clongowes and not the other way about. Belvedere was a much less impressive place to look at, smaller, more confined, poorer in historical associations and – in James Joyce's time – slightly in decline.

Fr Finlay's progressive term of office had been followed by three short incumbencies. He was immediately succeeded by Fr James Cullen, already a member of the community though not a teacher in the school. But, in the words of his biographer, his appointment 'cast him into profound misery', due to his sense of complete incapacity for the task, and he was duly relieved of it after only one year.[32] He was followed by young Fr Matthew Devitt in 1889, but he only stayed two years before replacing Fr Conmee in Clongowes. Fr Thomas Wheeler became Belvedere's third rector in four years, but strained relations with the provincial, Fr Kenny, led to his replacement by Fr William Henry in 1894. [33] In the previous twelve years, there had been seven different prefects of studies. Fr Henry's appointment in the double capacity of rector and prefect of studies brought this period of administrative instability to an end. But it had taken its toll. Fr Finlay remembered the roll as having reached 300 in his time.[34] By 1900, when Fr Henry left office, it had fallen to less than 200.[35] The Jesuit general expressed anxiety at what he saw as an inexplicable decline in his letter of 16 March 1897 to the provincial.[36] More than numbers suffered. Use of the playing-fields on the south side of the city, purchased by Fr Finlay, had been discontinued by Joyce's time.[37] Apart from the sodality, revived by Fr Cullen at Fr Finlay's request,[38] and the annual theatricals, there was little of what could be called extra-curricular activity in Belvedere while Joyce was there. In his final year, gymnastics was introduced by Fr Nicholas Tomkin, appointed minister in 1897.[39] Some indication of the state of things in the nineties can be had from an opinion long afterwards expressed by W. G. Fallon, one of Joyce's contemporaries. Fr Tomkin became rector in 1900 and he brought about such improvements in the situation that he could be said, in Fallon's view, to have 'resurrected

# Religious Exercises in College.

### EVERY DAY.
9.30 a.m. Mass.
12 a.m. Beads or Instruction.

### TUESDAYS.
9 a.m. Sodality of the Holy Angels.

### SATURDAYS.
9 a.m. Sodality meeting of Congregation of B.V.M.
10 to 12 a.m. Confessions.
12 a.m. Benediction of M. H. Sacrament.

### FIRST FRIDAY OF THE MONTH.
Benediction of the M. H. Sacrament.
ANNUAL FIRST COMMUNION on the Feast of the Sacred Heart.

### ANNUAL RETREAT
Beginning on the 6th October and ending on the 10th, Feast of St. Francis Borgia.

---

Parents are earnestly requested to co-operate, in the following particulars, with the Masters of the College :—

Where apparent remissness in the discharge of religious duties is observable, especially in the frequentation of the Sacraments, or attendance at daily Mass, the Superior is to be acquainted of it without delay.

If sufficient diligence be not shown in the performance of home-work, the Prefect of Studies is to be at once informed.

Apologies for school lessons, or absence from College, should not be sent without grave reason.

The Monthly-Judgment, which will be sent henceforward, will facilitate attention to these particulars. Parents are invited to sign it, and, if necessary, comment on it.

Part of the 1888 Prospectus. By Joyce's time the annual retreat had been moved to December, in preparation for the feast of Belvedere's patron, St Francis Xavier.

the College'.[40] It was to Belvedere in the valley period between the rectorships of Finlay and Tomkin that James and Stanislaus Joyce came.

The routine of a day-school like Belvedere was quite different from the regimented life of Clongowes.[41] The day began at 9.30 with Mass. As in Clongowes there were four classes a day, each lasting an hour. The morning classes began at 10. At midday, 'beads' were said in the chapel and then the boys ate their lunches in the garden – Stephen Dedalus and Vincent Heron talked together over theirs. Sometimes there might be an 'instruction' from the spiritual father, instead of beads at this time. Afternoon classes lasted from one till three. One of the punishments in Belvedere was to be kept in after three to do extra work.[42] Confessions were heard during the hours of class on Saturday mornings and school ended with benediction.[43]

His new school must have seemed strange enough to eleven-year old Joyce. But there were at least a few familiar faces. Apart from Fr Conmee, there was the minister, Fr Henry Fegan, who had been minister for two of Joyce's years in Clongowes. And there was also Mr Andrew Macardle, his former Third Line Prefect 'McGlade'. The rector in 1892–93 was Fr Thomas Wheeler. Joyce was to encounter him again in UCD between 1898 and 1901, and it is almost certainly he whom he describes in the final chapter of *A Portrait* as 'the portly florid bursar with his cap of grey hair' (456), a stickler for punctuality.[44] He was acting as prefect of studies for the year in Belvedere, as well as being rector, and the entry of James and Stanislaus Joyce, sons of John Stanislaus Joyce of 14 Fitzgibbon St, into Third Grammar and Elements respectively, is recorded in his hand.[45] The spiritual father was Fr James Cullen, who remained in that office throughout Joyce's time in the school and was to play a significant part in his development a few years later. There were six other priests and two brothers in the community that year, making a total of thirteen. Due to the 'transference of masters' which Stephen would discuss with polite indifference with another rector in his final year (413), the composition of the Belvedere community changed from year to year. But it always remained the same size. In addition to the Jesuits, there were also a number of laymen on the teaching staff, 'tutors', 'professors' or 'secular masters' as the ledgers variously describe them. The number varied – there were five when Joyce came to the school and only three when he was leaving. The most stable member of the lay-staff in Joyce's time, and the best paid, was George Dempsey. He received £12 a month.[46]

When Joyce returned to Belvedere in September 1893 to begin his first full year and prepare for the Intermediate examinations, he would have noticed several changes in the staff. There was a new

The Belvedere community in 1894, with the rector Fr Thomas Wheeler seated in the centre. The minister, Fr Charles Farley (mentioned in *Ulysses*) is seated, second from the left. Fr Richard Campbell ('Lantern Jaws' or 'Foxy Campbell') is standing, second from the left, and Mr Barrett is at the extreme right.

95

minister in the person of Fr Charles Farley. This is possibly the teacher disparaged by Stanislaus Joyce as 'scatter-brained Father Farrelly' [sic].[47] Leopold Bloom, passing All Hallows (better known as St Andrew's, Westland Row), regrets that he hadn't 'worked' Fr Conmee 'about getting Molly into the choir instead of that Father Farley who looked a fool but wasn't' (U 98).[48] On entering the Jesuits from Tullabeg in 1877, he had described himself disarmingly as 'rather backward'.[49] Fr Conmee, like Fr Fegan, was gone and his place in charge of the sodality had been taken by Fr Richard Campbell, 'Lantern Jaws' or 'Foxy Campbell' as the boys called him according to Joyce's recollection. It was his face, 'eyeless and sourfavoured and devout, shot with pink tinges of suffocated anger', a 'raw reddish glow . . . on the shaven gills', which came spontaneously to Stephen's mind at the thought of himself as a Jesuit (422).[50] Mr Macardle had been replaced by another of Joyce's former prefects in Clongowes, Mr Patrick Barrett. The new prefect of studies was Fr Thomas Maher. He remained only one year but his name turns up in Ulysses in a list of 'prominent members of the clergy' and others who applauded the citizen's singing (412). By 1904, like Fr Farley, he was a member of the Gardiner St community and Joyce may have picked his name more or less at random. But he may also have remembered the prefect of studies who had presided over his year in Preparatory Grade.[51]

School records in the nineties were not consistently maintained but Fr Maher, who held office for only one year, was better in this respect than most of his colleagues and we possess full class-lists for 1893–94. These lists contain the boys' full names, taken from their birth certificates, as well as dates of birth. They are not given in alphabetical order or order of seniority, but ranged against a series of numbers from one to fifty-four, with no names corresponding to numbers 1–8, 14–20 or 44–54 and in a sequence which it is now impossible to explain. Since the information is derived from birth certificates, the error in Joyce's birth certificate ('Augusta' for 'Augustine' as the second name) is reproduced in Fr Maher's list.[52] Someone had remembered to tell Fr Wheeler the previous year and his record of new boys has Joyce's full name correctly entered.

As the only one of Joyce's classes in Belvedere for which we have such a record, this list seems worth reproducing. Although Fr Maher did not include addresses, I have added these where they are known.[53] Eugene de Courcy Lawless, 17 August 1881, Bellevue, Sutton; James Augusta Joyce, 2 February 1882, 14 Fitzgibbon St; Leo John Wilkins, 9 June 1880, 2 Richmond Place, NCR; Edmund Hutchinson, 21 April 1881, 9 Merchants' Quay; Patrick Thomas Healy, 22 September 1880, 20 Upper Gardiner St; William David Joseph

Connolly, 23 July 1880; Alex Augustine Francis McDonald, 28 August 1881, 25 Merchants' Quay; Patrick Vincent Michael Ryan, 27 September 1881; Francis Gowan, 4 December 1880, Red Island, Skerries; William Joseph Deegan, 23 June 1880; Richard Sheehy, 1 January 1882, 11 Temple St; George Pope, 24 December 1880; John Aloysius Toner, 27 January 1882; William Gilbert Egan, 9 June 1881; Thomas St. Charles Leahy, 4 November 1880; Mathias Joseph Kelly, 2 June 1880, 64 Blessington St; John Joseph O'Neill, 21 November 1880, 67 Aughrim St; James Lenehan, 28 May 1881, Capel St; David Dominick O'Connell, 26 April 1881; Patrick Joseph Dwyer, 6 September 1880; Joseph Clarke, 20 January 1882; Kevin Delany, 1 March 1881; Laurence Joseph O'Neill, 14 August 1881, Kinsealy; Thomas Francis Mallon, 27 January 1881, Lower Castle Yard; Charles Paget O'Brien Butler, 18 July 1881, 8 Epworth Terrace, NCR; Edward Hyar, 30 July 1881; Robert McGovern 19 November 1881; Charles Edward Straker, 23 February 1882, 41 Wellington Rd.

Some of the names here are familiar. Lawless is in class to hear the rector announce the forthcoming retreat, when he is made the butt of Fr Henry's reminder that school will resume as usual after the retreat ends (134).[54] Dwyer is in the group of Stephen's school companions whom he stumbles across on the Bull Island (183).[55] Lenehan, a member of the well-known hardware firm in Capel St, may have lent at least his name to the character who turns up in 'Two Gallants' and *Ulysses*.[56] David O'Connell's father is John, described in the school register as 'Manager, Glasnevin Cemetery'. This is the decent, prosperously large 'caretaker' Bloom and his friends meet in the cemetery at Paddy Dignam's funeral.[57] Mallon's father, 'John Mallon of Lower Castle Yard' (*U* 749), accommodating assistant commissioner of Dublin Metropolitan Police, is mentioned in Bloom's conversation with Stephen in the cabman's shelter in the early hours.[58] Richard Sheehy is the elder of two brothers who were in Belvedere in Joyce's time, Eugene being the younger.[59] They are the sons of Mr David Sheehy MP, with whose wife Fr Conmee exchanges pleasantries in Mountjoy Square on his way out to Artane (*U* 280–81).[60] Later in his school career, Joyce was a regular visitor in their hospitable house. Leo Wilkins appears, with his brother Joe, in 'An Encounter' under the pseudonym of Leo Dillon, remembered as a fat, clumsy idler who funked a day's 'mitching' from school.[61]

Preparatory Grade is the only one of Joyce's classes for which a full list of pupils like this survives. Clearly, it does not include the names of all those associated with him in his time in Belvedere or associated by him with the school. Boys moved through the grades at different rates, depending on age and ability. Fr Maher noted at the top of the list given above that 'all boys born on or after June 1 '81 can go in for

97

Vincent Connolly, on whose appearance Joyce based his description of 'Heron', Connolly's younger brother Albrecht, in *A Portrait* (photograph taken in 1897).

Prep. Grade again in 1895'. This included Joyce, the second youngest in a class where some of the boys were almost two years his senior. Instead of repeating Preparatory, however (like Vincent Connolly a few years previously), Joyce moved on at once to Junior Grade. As a result he was too young to enter Middle Grade in 1895 and had to wait a year. Because of this system boys who did not start with him later became his more or less direct contemporaries. Two of these have a prominent place in the final chapter of *A Portrait* and in *Ulysses*. J. F. Byrne, 'Cranly' in the novels, was born on 11 February 1880 and entered Belvedere on 3 September 1892. He did Junior Grade in 1894 and was presumably repeating this examination in 1895 when he and Joyce shared the same classroom.[62] Vincent Cosgrave ('Lynch') was older again, having been born on 22 November 1877, but he only came to Belvedere on 28 November 1892. He was in Junior Grade in the year before Byrne.[63] Both left Belvedere in 1895 and went to UCD.[64] Neither of these close friends of the university years appears in the Belvedere chapters.[65]

Joyce mentions the names of ten of his Belvedere companions. The most significant is evidently the boy he calls 'Heron', his friend and rival in school, whose bird-like physical appearance is described in detail. According to Richard Ellmann, this character, Vincent Heron in full, is a composite of the two Connolly brothers Vincent and Albrecht. The personality and attire belong to Albrecht, who was Joyce's direct contemporary; the physical features are those of his elder brother Vincent.[66] 'The fop of Belvedere College', as Ellmann reports,[67] with his cane and Norfolk coat, something of Connolly's foppishness seems to have been transferred to his companion Wallis, whom Stephen encounters him with on the night of the Whitsuntide play. From the context it appears that Wallis is not himself a member of the college.[68] The rivalry between Heron and Dedalus is always an element in their relationship. On the night of the play and in the incident on the Clonliffe Road two years before, this rivalry is obvious enough. But even in the catechism class, as the boys anticipate how Stephen will be able to sidetrack the rector with questions when he arrives, Heron jealously 'checks' their talk from time to time (357). And in the middle of Stephen's retreat crisis, Vincent Heron's innocuous conversation with Mr Tate about the weather makes Stephen's spiritual anguish stand out in even sharper relief. Heron may be said to win this round but Stephen has the last word. He comes upon a group of his schoolfellows swimming off the Bull, among them Connolly (now given his real name). Their adolescent horseplay and heavy-handed banter incurs his secret contempt as he himself strides high-mindedly towards his destiny.

Connolly is accompanied on this occasion by three others, Shuley, Ennis and Dwyer. Dwyer, as we have seen, was in Joyce's class from the beginning. James Shuley, who wore a 'deep unbuttoned collar' (430), came to the school in 1889 and was in Rudiments with Albrecht Connolly in 1890.[69] The Belvedere *Cash Book* records regular payments during Joyce's years for Peter Paul Ennis. Having heard earlier of his blundering stupidity in mathematics class, we are told of how 'characterless' he looks on the Bull 'without his scarlet belt with the snaky clasp' (430). Of the two boys who join Heron in bullying Stephen about his literary opinions, Nash may be a real person (the name occurs once in the *Cash Book*)[70] while the other, Boland, seems to be a pseudonym. Why Joyce used pseudonyms in some cases and not others is hardly more clear for Belvedere than for Clongowes. Both Boland and Nash appear in an unpleasant light but Nash, described in circumstantial detail, is perhaps even more contemptible than Boland. The three other boys mentioned have real names. Lawless has been referred to already, another of Joyce's contemporaries from his days in the Preparatory Grade. Tallon was a very common name in the school at the time. The *Prefect of Studies' Book* contains four between 1890 and 1893. One of these, Justin Joseph, almost two years younger than Joyce, came to the school just the day before him in 1893 and went into Elements with Stanislaus. It is possible that he is Bertie, 'the little boy who had to dance the sunbonnet dance by himself' on the evening of the play (322).[71] Finally, William Fallon, the boy 'with a silly laugh' who had noticed how often the Dedaluses moved house (424), entered Elements in September 1891.[72]

The Joyces were not the only ones on the move in those years. The Sheehys had three different addresses in James Joyce's time at Belvedere: Temple St, Eccles St, and Belvedere Place. But the Joyces' transfers from Fitzgibbon St, to Drumcondra, back to North Richmond St (where the two eldest boys had been briefly at school), and out to 'the sloblands of Fairview' (438), were an index of social decline. Hence Stephen's defensive reaction to what may have been an innocent question on Fallon's part. Most of the boys at that time lived in the immediate proximity of the college. This now rather depressed neighbourhood had not yet 'gone down'. Others lived (as do the majority of Belvedere boys today) in the fashionable suburbs on the edge of the city.[73] But they did not all have 'good addresses' and, as the Belvedere accounts make clear, the Joyces were not the only ones in straitened circumstances.[74] Whatever Stephen may have read into Fallon's question, Belvedere seems to have been free of the snobbery he thought he had met among 'the Clongowes gentry' (*U* 49). James Joyce was always a welcome guest in the home of Richard and Eugene Sheehy, whose father was a Westminster MP.[75]

There were at least two other MPs with sons in the school at this period. T. D. Sullivan, like Sheehy an anti-Parnellite after the split, sent his son Christopher Joseph to Belvedere in 1889. He was in Junior Grade with Vincent Connolly and Vincent Cosgrave in 1892–93. The Sheehys and Sullivans conform to the image of Jesuit schools in this period as institutions peopled exclusively by 'Castle Catholics'.[76] The third MP's son fits less easily into this stereotype. Charles Stuart [*sic*] Parnell Clancy, who was in Elements in 1889–90 with Albrecht Connolly and for whom fees were still being paid in 1896, was the son of J. J. Clancy of 53 Rutland Square. His political allegiance was not misrepresented by the name he had given his son.[77] It is worth remarking that this boy is not to be confused with Charles Boyce Clancy. He seems to have been the son of 'Long John' Clancy, the sub-sheriff of Dublin, who appears under his own name or disguised as 'Long John Fanning' in *Dubliners* and the later works, but not in *A Portrait*.[78]

Gorman is probably right about the smallness of Belvedere and the closeness of its community life.[79] Not merely were the numbers relatively small but the spaces in which they moved were confined. Joyce is likely to have known, in some measure, all those who were there in his time. If it was embarassing that some of your school-

The Sheehy brothers, Eugene and Richard, shown among the gymnasts in the Whitsuntide entertainment in Belvedere, 1898.

fellows noticed how often you changed your abode or carried tales about your father's bankruptcy into school,[80] it may have been worse to be at school with the son of your father's creditor. It was in his year in the Preparatory Grade that James accompanied his father to Cork, to sell off what remained of the family property there and so be able to pay his debts to Reuben Dodd.[81] Reuben Dodd Jr was actually in class with Joyce, who avenged himself and his father by snubbing his classmate and laughing uproariously at his solecisms in Mr Dempsey's class.[82]

George Dempsey must already have been something of an institution in the school when Joyce first encountered him in Preparatory Grade. Dempsey had begun his association with the college on 27 August 1884, the day on which Fr Finlay's new building had been opened,[83] and his long list of Intermediate successes, among whom Joyce was to be numbered, had already begun.[84] He was to continue teaching until 1923, a career of almost forty years which was quite unparalleled by any other teacher, Jesuit or lay. Mr Dempsey's subject, under Intermediate regulations, embraced not only English but also history and geography.[85] Thus, in *A Portrait*, 'the English lesson began with the hearing of the history' (381). In this way, as his most successful student of all, Arthur Cox, wrote on the occasion of his retirement, he had 'the most important scope of any teacher save those concerned with Divine things'. It was undoubtedly true, as Cox added, that 'his influence through so many years ... has been enormous and far-reaching upon the vast numbers of students who passed through his care'.[86]

J. F. Byrne remembered Dempsey as resembling Justice Oliver Wendell Holmes.[87] Eugene Sheehy wrote a more extended description:

> Mr Dempsey was a rather tall, thin man of about fifty years of age and, save that he walked with a slight stoop, presented the appearance of a retired military officer. He had thin, grey hair and a hay-coloured moustache, one side of which became pointed as the result of the undue attention of his right hand, whilst the left side remained tousled and untidy.[88]

William Dawson, who was some four years older than Joyce and who sat in Junior Grade in 1893 with Cosgrave and Vincent Connolly, recalled Mr Dempsey's class in Middle Grade:

> The class was usually held between 1 and 2 p.m., an excellent period, coming, as it did, after the pangs of hunger had been appeased, and before the feverish unrest, which the end of the day always produces, had commenced to make itself felt. Mr Dempsey

seated himself on a chair before the front desk – he disdained the giddy eminence of the throne – and after a jovial, perhaps slightly sarcastic greeting to his pupils, proceeded to sound the depths of their ignorance. It was part of the settled procedure that each text-book was brought in by a separate youth, and we in the front desk had the task of submitting these in turn to the Professor. It was a glorious position. We felt like Cabinet Ministers. The fortunes of the class were in our hands. Hoarse whispers or scraps of paper frequently reached us from 'the backwoodsmen', praying that history might be put on next, or entreating that the geography might be delayed. Then there were exhibitioners in our Cabinet, and it was felt that a timely word from them might serve to avert a crisis in the class.[89]

At least in Junior Grade, by which time he was an exhibitioner, Joyce sat 'near the window in the front desk of the left row, facing the teacher, and immediately under the dais'.[90] This might have had something to do with his eyesight, but it probably also reflected his academic position in the class.[91]

For Stephen Dedalus, whose English teacher is called Mr Tate, 'the essay . . . was the chief labour of his week' (327). On his way to school on Tuesday mornings, he would wonder whether or not he would be first. The essay loomed large in the minds of most of Dempsey's pupils, though for many of the others the issue was not whether they would be first but whether they would be the target of the teacher's dreaded sarcasm.[92] In the English class on Tuesday, as J. F. Byrne recounts,

a few of the 'composers' would be asked by Dempsey to read their lucubrations, and among these James Joyce was one of the most frequently called upon. Joyce was a good reader, and while he read, Dempsey would literally wiggle and chuckle with delight.

The reaction of the class had also to be considered:

Generally, the class, too, liked Joyce's efforts, but there were occasions when the floridity of his stuff made you feel as if you were in the hot-house out in the Botanic Gardens.[93]

On one occasion, Stephen's (and Joyce's) essay was highlighted by the teacher for reasons other than literary excellence: it contained doctrinal error. In the novel, Mr Tate's charge hushed the class and acutely embarrassed Stephen Dedalus.

A short laugh from Mr Tate set the Class more at ease.
– Perhaps you didn't know that, he said.
– Where? asked Stephen.

Mr George Dempsey in 1910.

Mr Tate [...] spread out the essay.
– Here. It's about the Creator and the soul. Rrm . . .
rrm . . . rrm . . . . Ah! *without a possibility of ever approaching nearer*. That's heresy.

Stephen murmured:
– I meant *without a possibility of ever reaching*.

It was a submission and Mr Tate, appeased, folded up the essay and passed it across to him saying:
– O . . . . Ah! *ever reaching*. That's another story (328).

For Heron and his friends, this was an ideal opportunity to pull their precocious classmate down a peg or two. The incident on the Clonliffe Road a few nights after the Tuesday class, in which his brother was bullied by the other three for his literary as well as his theological errors, was 'one of the unpleasantest memories' of this period, according to Stanislaus, who vouches for its accuracy.[94]

Fifteen years later, Dempsey's teaching was criticised by an inspector from the Intermediate Education Board, with less appreciation than he might have had for the merits of memorising verse at a receptive age:

> The pupils (in Junior Grade) were made to repeat about twenty lines of the 'Morte d'Arthur' which they had learnt by heart. Difficult words were explained. The *Middle* Grade boys were doing Milton's 'L'Allegro', which was treated in the same manner. Although this type of teaching may enable the pupils to gain high marks in an examination, it is hardly calculated to give them a taste for literature, or a wider outlook. The teacher should encourage the class to go beyond the limits of the text-book, and should try to open the minds of the boys to a wider appreciation of literature.

As in English, Mr Dempsey's teaching of geography 'partook too largely of the nature of "coaching"'. In history, 'the teacher ... should discuss the subject with his class in a broad manner, not confining his exposition merely to dry facts'.[95] Curiously, it is the consensus of his pupils that this is exactly what Mr Dempsey did. Arthur Cox, who had just left Belvedere when the inspection was made, observed:

> Year after year examination results testified to his professional capacity; no less frequently his past pupils showed in some better way their affection and esteem. History, and particularly Irish history, he made a thing of life and actuality; Literature ceased to be a question of books and broadened out to meet the confines of thought and experience; geography became converted from a dull affair of names and lists into what it really is, the science of all peoples and of the world. He was a great educator, and approached more nearly to the best ideal of the University professor than the mere school teacher.[96]

William Dawson remembered how he had first seen *Hamlet* on the stage because Mr Dempsey had encouraged him to go and how the teacher was always ready to advise his pupils on the books they should read.[97] Edward Freeman wrote in an obituary:

> Few of us who were privileged in being taught by George Dempsey will ever forget him. He was an excellent teacher and had the faculty of making his subject always interesting. His fund of anecdotes and illustrations and his oft-repeated 'Day you see?' kept

the wandering mind attentive and alert. The fact that he held attention and interest was proved by that crucial schoolboy test – his hour passed quickly.[98]

The ineptitude of the inspector's remarks, even allowing for some exaggeration on the part of eulogists, is very clear.

Joyce's picture of Dempsey, as Mr Tate, is brief but respectful. English was naturally the subject most to his taste and Dempsey's literary culture and breadth of mind were bound to appeal to him. In querying the orthodoxy of Stephen's essay, Mr Tate displays a notable degree of theological sophistication. But there is also, perhaps, a hint of good-humoured scepticism faintly discernible in the conversation Stephen overhears between the English teacher and Vincent Heron.[99] George Dempsey usually did not send boys out to be pandied; he preferred to spur on the recalcitrant with a little sarcasm.[100] 'Gussie' Joyce, as the teacher jocularly called him,[101] was not in need of such stimulation. Byrne could see that Dempsey 'liked him a great deal' and 'for his own sake, just as much as for his proficiency in English'.[102] Gorman and Stanislaus Joyce both testify to the fact that teacher and pupil remained in contact in later years, with Dempsey forwarding books of reference to Joyce and urging publication of his verse in *The Belvederian*.[103] Of all the intellectual influences on James Joyce in school, whether in Clongowes or Belvedere, George Dempsey seems to have been the most significant.

While he was reading Lamb's *Adventures of Ulysses* with Mr Dempsey and studying Lyster's selection of English poets, which included Byron ('Childe Harold's Good Night' and 'The Gladiator') but not Tennyson,[104] Joyce was also preparing for the Intermediate in Latin, French, Italian and mathematics (arithmetic, algebra and Euclid). We know much less about who his other teachers were. J. F. Byrne thought that, in his time, 'none of the clerical teachers in Belvedere was deserving of a high rating as a teacher'.[105] Fr Wheeler, the rector, has been described as 'one of the Irish Province's most gifted masters of the last century'. Like most of his fellows-Jesuits at the time, he had pursued the greater part of his studies for the priesthood abroad: in France, Belgium and Spain.[106] But we cannot be sure whether he ever taught Joyce. He was taught Italian in this year by a Mr Loup, who spent only the year in Belvedere. Afterwards he went to Clongowes where he was 'rather a sheep fallen amongst wolves'.[107] But he was one of the teachers Joyce remembered (if only, perhaps, for his suggestive name) when Gorman asked him about his 'instructors' years later.[108] George Dempsey's brother-in-law P. Bertram Foy taught physics (or 'natural philosophy') and chemistry, neither of which James Joyce took up until the following year. But, if

Examinations in progress in the school theatre in Belvedere in 1907. This is where Joyce did his public examinations. Mr Dempsey is standing, second from left.

Fr Campbell's memory – or the records on which he drew – many years later can be relied on,[109] Foy also taught junior mathematics and may have had Joyce in his class in 1893–94. Alternatively, his teacher may have been Michael McCluskey, another layman on the staff, who shared responsibility for 'science' (including mathematics) with Foy at the time.[110]

In the early 1890s, Belvedere, along with numerous other Irish schools, submitted pupils for the examinations of the Department of Science and Art, based in South Kensington.[111] This was in addition to the ordinary Intermediate examinations. The general aim of the Department of Science and Art was 'to help science teaching throughout Great Britain and Ireland'.[112] Grants were offered on the basis of school organisation and, like the Intermediate, on results. To qualify, schools had to organise themselves formally and provide a minimum of thirteen hours teaching a week in science subjects (including mathematics). James Joyce was one of fifty-six boys from the different grades in Belvedere who were entered for the mathematics examination, held on Wednesday 9 May 1894. Apart from older pupils in higher grades like Byrne and Cosgrave, contemporaries of Joyce like Albrecht Connolly and Reuben Dodd also sat the examination. But only two of the boys actually listed with Joyce in the Preparatory Grade for that year, Francis Gowan and Patrick Healy, were among the other candidates. The examination was held, like all public examinations (then and for many years afterwards) in the theatre. It was supervised by Fr Wheeler, Mr Macardle (who came over for the occasion from Milltown Park, where he was studying theology), and three laymen from outside the college.[113] An inspector, Major J. E. Campbell R.E., came while the examination was on and stayed for an hour. After the formalities of this, his first major academic test, Joyce may have been glad to find diversion at the 'Araby' bazaar which came to Dublin the following week, from 14 to 19 May.[114] He may not have been the only visitor from Belvedere. An entry in the *Cash Book* records that someone spent £2 there on 17 May.

The Intermediate began a few weeks later on 12 June.[115] The Latin examination was held that day and the other subjects occupied the rest of the week, with two three-hour papers (from 10 to 1 and from 3 to 6) on most days. Italian was in the middle of the second week; then Joyce was free for the summer. English was on the second day. In the morning he had to write a composition and answer questions on grammar and Lyster's selection of poetry. The choice of compositions was as follows:

(a) 'There is a pleasure in the pathless woods,
    There is a rapture on the lonely shore'.

108

(Deal with this by describing a ramble through a wood, or along the seashore).

(b) Describe an imaginary balloon voyage.

(c) Compare a life of idleness with a life of activity and work.

This was the only question in which candidates had a choice – they were to do one out of three. Joyce's favourite poet turned up in the last section of the paper, along with Cowper, Wordsworth and Southey: 'Why does Byron call on the Goths to arise and glut their ire?' Like this one on 'The Gladiator', the other poetry questions appealed exclusively to powers of memory and comprehension, leaving little scope for literary appreciation. In the afternoon Joyce had to address himself to Lamb's *Adventures of Ulysses*, chapters I–VII. There were five questions, all of them factual and prosaic and leaving little scope for the reader's fantasy:

1. Mention the circumstances in which Ulysses revealed his name to Alcinous, and state the country of which he was in search.
2. Give a brief outline of the means adopted by Ulysses and his companions to escape from the cave of the Cyclops.
3. Indicate the pronunciation of the following proper names by marking the long vowels thus –, and the short ones thus ᴗ: Cocytus, Penelope, Bootes, Menelaus, Alcinous, Cythera.
4. Mention a peculiar prejudice of the Phaecians about whips, and the incident from which it arose.
5. In what circumstances did Ulysses exact an oath from his companions, and what was its nature?

After that, there were questions about 'English and Irish History to A.D. 1899' (which were almost exclusively about England) and geography. These latter sections carried 450 of the 600 marks assigned to the paper.[116] It is tempting to speculate that Joyce's relatively modest mark in English might have been due to his spending too long at the first section of the afternoon paper.

During the summer holidays, James went on a trip to Glasgow with his father. His mother was pregnant again but the child died before the summer was out or early in the autumn, a few weeks after birth.[117] Some time afterwards – 'probably late in 1894', according to Ellmann's estimate – the family, now lurching from one crisis to another, moved house again. This time they went back into the city, to 17 North Richmond St, where the two older boys had briefly attended school in the spring of 1893 and where Joyce set his story 'Araby'.[118] The Kensington results were announced on 1 August and showed that Joyce had passed, but not sufficiently well to base a claim for payment on his result. The new school year would have begun before the Intermediate results came out (in the first two weeks of

| Examination Number | STUDENT'S NAME AND ADDRESS | Greek |
|---|---|---|
| | MAXIMUM .. | 1200 |
| 1041 | Jackson, Thomas, Grammar School, Drogheda | x |
| 1042 | Jackson, Thomas, Educational Institution, Dundalk | x |
| 1043 | [Failed] | x |
| 1044 | Johnson, Christopher A., Presentation College, Mardyke, Cork | x |
| 1045 | Johnston, Francis P., Clongowes Wood College (s. j.), Sallins | x |
| 1046 | Johnston, James E., Intermediate School, Armagh | 10 |
| 1047 | Jones, Christopher F., Merchant Taylors' Sch.,Wellington qy.,Dublin | x |
| 1048 | [Failed] | f |
| 1049 | Jones, Francis, Christian Schools, Dundalk | x |
| 1050 | [Failed] | x |
| 1051 | [Failed] | x |
| 1052 | Jordan, Hugh, Christian Schools, Newry | x |
| 1053 | Jordan, Simon F., Christian Schools, Drogheda | x |
| 1054 | [Failed] | x |
| 1055 | Joyce, James A., Belvedere College (s. j.), Dublin | x |
| 1056 | [Failed] | x |
| 1057 | Judge, Thomas M., Rockwell College, Cashel | x |
| 1058 | Kahn, Peter, St. Mary's College (s. m.), Dundalk | x |
| 1059 | [Failed] | x |
| 1060 | [Failed] | x |
| 1061 | Kavanagh, John J., Christian Schools, N. Richmond street, Dublin | x |
| 1062 | Kavanagh, Joseph, Christian Schools, Dingle | x |
| 1063 | [Failed] | x |
| 1064 | [Failed] | x |
| 1065 | Kavanagh, William, Christian Schs., St. Vincent's Orph., Glasnevin | x |
| 1066 | [Not Examined] | x |
| 1067 | Kealy, Michael, Christian Schools, Gorey | x |
| 1068 | [Failed] | x |
| 1069 | [Not Examined] | x |
| 1070 | Keating, James J., Christian Schools, Newry | x |
| 1071 | [Failed] | x |
| 1072 | Keeffe, Michael, Christian Schools, New Ross | x |
| 1073 | Keeffe, Thomas, Christian Schools, Charleville | 380 |
| 1074 | [Not Examined] | x |
| 1075 | Keegan, Michael, Christian Schools, Westland row, Dublin | x |
| 1076 | Keegan, Richard, Christian Schools, Westland row, Dublin | x |
| 1077 | Keelan, John, Christian Schools, Mullingar | x |
| 1078 | Kehoe, James F., St. Mary's College (s. m.), Dundalk | 600 |
| 1079 | [Failed] | x |
| 1080 | Keleher, John, Christian Schools, Cork | x |

Joyce's Intermediate results, 1894.

| Latin | English | French | German | Italian | Celtic | Arithmetic | Euclid | Algebra | Drawing | Total under Rule 38 | Examination Number |
|---|---|---|---|---|---|---|---|---|---|---|---|
| 1200 | 1200 | 700 | 700 | 500 | 600 | 600 | 600 | 600 | 300 | | |
| 145 | 240 | f | × | × | × | 145 | 120 | f | f | 650 | 1041 |
| 160 | 270 | 205 | × | × | × | 155 | 115 | f | f | 905 | 1042 |
| × | f | f | × | × | × | 25 | f | × | 35 | 60 | 1043 |
| × | 160 | 119 | × | × | × | 145 | 25 | f | f | 449 | 1044 |
| 15 | 105 | × | × | × | × | 290 | 90 | 90 | × | 590 | 1045 |
| 195 | 305 | × | × | × | × | 350 | 140 | 65 | × | 1065 | 1046 |
| 105 | 370 | 257 | × | × | × | 470 | 225 | 265 | f | 1692 | 1047 |
| f | 205 | × | × | × | × | f | 30 | f | × | 235 | 1048 |
| × | 100 | 180 | × | × | × | 270 | P | P | 25 | 575 | 1049 |
| f | 160 | × | × | × | × | 200 | f | f | P | 360 | 1050 |
| × | 180 | f | × | × | × | 150 | f | × | 75 | 405 | 1051 |
| × | 455 | 388 | 68 | 163 | 266 | 480 | 295 | 380 | × | 2495 | 1052 |
| × | P | 61 | × | × | × | 160 | 150 | f | f | 371 | 1053 |
| f | 425 | f | × | × | × | 320 | 190 | f | f | 935 | 1054 |
| 700 | 455 | 400 | × | 211 | × | 430 | 230 | 130 | × | 2556 | 1055 |
| f | 245 | × | × | × | × | 185 | 50 | f | × | 480 | 1056 |
| 5 | 130 | 118 | × | × | × | 275 | f | 10 | × | 538 | 1057 |
| 45 | 345 | 125 | × | × | × | 340 | 200 | P | × | 1053 | 1058 |
| × | f | 32 | × | × | × | f | 95 | f | f | 127 | 1059 |
| × | f | 49 | × | × | × | 155 | P | f | f | 204 | 1060 |
| × | 225 | 157 | × | × | × | 245 | f | 80 | f | 707 | 1061 |
| × | 20 | f | × | × | 123 | 75 | P | × | P | 218 | 1062 |
| × | f | 25 | × | × | × | 235 | 20 | f | f | 280 | 1063 |
| × | f | f | × | × | × | 70 | f | × | f | 70 | 1064 |
| 225 | 530 | 460 | × | × | × | 520 | 290 | 230 | f | 2255 | 1065 |
| × | × | × | × | × | × | × | × | × | × | × | 1066 |
| × | 325 | 388 | × | × | × | 200 | 95 | × | f | 1008 | 1067 |
| × | 40 | f | × | × | × | 125 | f | × | 25 | 190 | 1068 |
| × | × | × | × | × | × | × | × | × | × | × | 1069 |
| × | 275 | 158 | f | f | 48 | 245 | 270 | 250 | × | 1246 | 1070 |
| × | f | 141 | × | × | × | 140 | 130 | 160 | f | 571 | 1071 |
| f | 280 | 99 | × | × | 7 | 175 | 20 | f | 15 | 596 | 1072 |
| × | 300 | 251 | × | × | × | 260 | 145 | × | × | 1586 | 1073 |
| 250 | × | × | × | × | × | × | × | × | × | × | 1074 |
| × | 450 | 289 | × | × | 10 | 550 | 190 | 170 | × | 1659 | 1075 |
| f | 385 | 286 | × | × | 25 | 470 | 240 | 80 | × | 1516 | 1076 |
| 30 | 445 | 243 | × | × | × | 165 | 205 | × | 15 | 1073 | 1077 |
| × | 410 | 368 | × | × | × | 400 | 280 | × | × | 2633 | 1078 |
| 575 | 150 | f | × | × | × | 110 | 20 | f | f | 280 | 1079 |
| × | 50 | 52 | × | × | × | 390 | 30 | × | f | 522 | 1080 |

111

September). His best mark of all was in arithmetic (400 out of 500), which explains why he had put in that year for the Kensington examination in the subject. This very good mark compensated for relatively poor totals in Euclid and especially algebra (230 and 130 out of 600, respectively). Apart from arithmetic, his best mark was in Latin, where, as well as the usual questions in grammar and composition and unseen translation common to all language papers, he had translated prepared selections from Caesar's *de Bello Gallico* and the poetry of Ovid and written about early Republican history. He got 700 out of a possible 1200. His English mark, at 455 out of 1200, was relatively low. In French, where the texts were Mme de Pressense's *Seulette* and Florian's *Fables,* he got 400 out of 700. His lowest mark among the languages was for Italian, where he had had to translate De Amicis' text *Cuore.* He got 211 out of 500. The Latin mark gained him a £2 prize and his aggregate was high enough to win an exhibition. He had come 103rd in Preparatory Grade, in which 132 exhibitions were awarded in 1894. It may have been October, as *A Portrait* suggests in reference to one of the years when he was successful,[119] before the £20 which his exhibition was worth was collected from the Bank of Ireland in College Green. It was promptly dissipated in a manner characteristic of father and son all their lives.[120]

Beginning Junior Grade with the new status of exhibitioner, Joyce would have found further changes in the staff, one at least of which was to be significant for him. Fr Wheeler was gone, his place taken by Fr William Henry, who combined the office of prefect of studies with that of rector from the beginning. Mr Barrett had also gone, thus breaking the one remaining link with Clongowes, for the time being at least. He, like Mr Macardle the year before, had been the only scholastic in the Belvedere community since Joyce arrived. Now there were three, including Mr Francis Ryan whom Joyce remembered (not kindly) as his teacher of French and who probably also taught him Italian.[121] Ryan was ordained at the end of this year and remained on the staff until 1897. Mr Loup was gone too.

William Henry, variously referred to as 'the rector' or 'the director' but never given his own name in *A Portrait,* was only thirty-five when he came to Belvedere in the autumn of 1894. Like Fr Conmee and Fr Devitt, he was a young rector. He had served his apprenticeship as a scholastic in Belvedere under Fr Finlay and been prefect of studies for two years. He was a native of Draperstown, Co. Derry and came from a large Catholic family[122] – there are no grounds for the common view that he was a 'convert', fanatical or otherwise.[123] He had been educated by the English Jesuits in Chesterfield, with his brother Denis, who afterwards became the first Lord Chief Justice of

Northern Ireland.[124] This was a somewhat surprising appointment for a Catholic and may help to explain why it was thought that the Jesuit Henry could hardly be of the same persuasion as Sir Denis. His fellow-Jesuits spoke of him as 'a hardheaded, solid little man', 'a tough nut', and they told the story of how he had made trial of various meditation books and then chosen one (Avencinus), to which he stuck for the rest of his life.[125] He was one of those precise, methodical, shrewd, but also perhaps slightly wooden men on whom superiors feel they can rely completely. One of his obituarists referred to Fr Henry's 'union of stern purpose in time of silence, and of fun at recreation', as a novice, which 'stamped him all through life'.[126] There is a suggestion of strain here, which sharply differentiates him from Fr Conmee. The impression of severity which is spoken of by his colleagues is echoed in Stephen's reference to the rector's 'shrewd harsh face' (358) and 'dark stern eyes' (360). But the same man who could report his anxieties about Joyce's behaviour to his parents could also laugh at the boy's public imitation of his mannerisms and later invite him to think of becoming a Jesuit. Joyce told Herbert Gorman that 'in spite of his harsh and warped character he was a man of breeding and not of the Father Daly class'. In the end, according to himself, Joyce 'got on . . . very well' with Fr Henry.[127]

In Stephen Dedalus' odyssey, 'the director' seemed to personify dangerous forces, 'the priestly denial of the senses',[128] which he felt he must reject. For him, the invitation to priesthood is a seduction. This may be why Fr Henry, as the representative of powers which threaten to swallow Stephen's individuality, has no name in the novel, only a title. Joyce himself would have had more mixed, less defined feelings towards the rector of Belvedere. While keeping the suspicious Stephen at his distance, he himself provides a surprisingly detailed description of what Fr Henry was like. We know that he has a 'shrewd northern face' (441) and that he speaks in a 'pedantic bass' (324). His mannered intonation is imitated by Heron. As he speaks, he clasps his hands. We hear his heavy witticism aimed at Lawless and his inspirational address to the class about the retreat and the college patron, St Francis Xavier. And we listen in the parlour to his grave small talk and his carefully weighed invitation to Stephen to become a Jesuit. Although he is distanced by the lack of a personal name, we actually see and hear more of Fr Henry than almost any other character in the novel. Of the Jesuits Stephen encountered while at school, some may make a more vivid impression on the reader but few have been more fully described.

William Henry was by training a classicist and taught Latin and Greek in Belvedere.[129] Joyce had chosen Italian in preference to Greek the year before [130] but studied Latin with Fr Henry, possibly from

Joseph Wilkins, 'Joe Dillon' in 'An Encounter': 'Everyone was incredulous when it was reported that he had a vocation for the priesthood. Nevertheless it was true.'

Junior Grade upwards. The rector taught religious knowledge to the senior classes, as the novel records, but he seems to have made a deeper impression, on Stephen and Joyce alike, in Latin class. In his 'Trieste Notebook', Joyce made two entries under the heading 'Henry', both of which eventually found their way into *A Portrait* and both of which recalled the rector as Latinist:

> In translating Ovid he spoke of porkers and potsherds and of chines of bacon.
> When I listen I can still hear him reading sonorously:
> *In tanto discrimine .... Implere ollam denariorum .... India mittit ebur.*[131]

It seems likely that, whatever other feelings Joyce may have had about Fr Henry, as a teacher of Latin he respected him.

J. F. Byrne has given a highly circumstantial account of the Junior Grade classroom which he and Joyce shared in 1894–95.[132] Apart from this, the only other echo of Joyce's life in school for this year is contained in his story 'An Encounter'. The reference to 'Mr Ryan' helps to fix the date of this incident, the truth of which is once more guaranteed by Stanislaus.[133] 'Mr Ryan' became 'Fr Ryan' in the summer and Joyce did not err on such points. The Dillons, as noted above, are in reality the Wilkins brothers – Joseph Wilkins was a few years older than Leo. Mahony's identity remains a mystery, but Fr Butler is evidently Fr Henry, as Ellmann has noted.[134] The 'mitchers' (in reality James and Stanislaus) did not, as they feared, meet him at the Pigeon House. Perhaps it is just as well – another boy had left from Rudiments at Christmas a few years before at the then rector's wish and the *Prefect of Studies' Book* supplied the reason: 'mitching'.

This 'break out of the weariness of school life' in the first week of June[135] was, in Joyce's case, a mere moment of respite after another hard year of work. The Intermediate began a fortnight later on Monday 17 June. This time he added natural philosophy and chemistry, studied under Mr Foy, to the subjects he had taken the year before. The English compositions offered him in 1895 were:[136]

(a) What profession or business would you like to adopt, and why?
(b) The importance of trifles.
(c) 'Slow rises Worth by Poverty depressed'.

The last title must surely have caught, and probably held, his eye. In addition, there were questions of the usual kind on the two set texts, Scott's *The Lord of the Isles* (Cantos I–III) and Defoe's *Robinson Crusoe*, more geography and 'English and Irish History – A.D. 1399 to 1603'. The Latin course included *de Bello Gallico* V and *Aeneid* V; the Roman history questions were about the period from the Punic Wars down to the Gracchi. In French, Joyce's class had read Xavier de Maistre's *La jeune Sibérienne* and Lamartine's *Bernard de Palissy*, as well as more of Florian's *Fables*. In Italian, there was more of *Cuore* and Metastasio's *Gioas Re di Giuda*. Joyce's results in the scientific subjects he had taken on were disastrous: he obtained a mere 20 per cent of the 500 marks available in each.[137] He also lost ground heavily in the mathematics subjects. Latin was slightly down, French and Italian slightly up. In English, he had improved by almost 100 marks. His result overall was just enough to put him among the exhibitioners, 164th out of 164. It was worth £20, this time tenable for three years. Joyce was now established as a 'winner' in the Intermediate stakes and this attracted the attention of the Dominicans. Two of them called to his home,

| Examination Number | STUDENT'S NAME AND ADDRESS | Greek | Latin | English | Commercial English | French |
|---|---|---|---|---|---|---|
| MAXIMUM .. | | 1200 | 1200 | 1200 | 400 | 700 |
| 3821 | Jones, Christopher F., Merchant Taylors' Sch., Wellington qy., Dublin | × | 294 | 395 | 35 | 343 |
| 3822 | [Failed] | × | × | 7 | × | 3 |
| 3823 | Jones, James E., Educational Institution, Dundalk | × | f | 255 | 20 | 568 |
| 3824 | Jones, Sidney F., Avoca School, Blackrock | 299 | 159 | 200 | × | 254 |
| 3825 | Jones, Webb B., Portora Royal School, Enniskillen | × | f | 185 | × | 65 |
| 3826 | [Failed] | × | × | 50 | × | f |
| 3827 | [Failed] | × | f | f | × | 21 |
| 3828 | Jordan, Hugh, Christian Schools, Newry [**P Ex.'94**] | × | × | 225 | × | 219 |
| 3829 | Joyce, James A., Belvedere College (s. J.), Dublin [**P.Ex.'94**] | × | 636 | 540 | × | 410 |
| 3830 | [Failed] | × | f | 27 | × | × |
| 3831 | [Failed] | × | × | 15 | × | f |
| 3832 | [Failed] | × | f | 25 | × | f |
| 3833 | Judge, Maurice J., Blackrock College, co. Dublin | × | f | 180 | × | 57 |
| 3834 | Judge, Thomas M., Rockwell College, Cashel | × | 174 | 60 | × | 221 |
| 3835 | Kane, John J., Christian Schools, Tipperary | 256 | 40 | 340 | × | 200 |
| 3836 | [Failed] | × | × | f | × | f |
| 3837 | Kavanagh, Jeremiah M., Christian Schs., N. Richmond st., Dublin | × | 255 | 360 | × | 310 |
| 3838 | Kavanagh, John J., Christian Schs., N. Richmond st., Dublin | × | × | 62 | f | 222 |
| 3839 | Kavanagh, Patrick, Christian Schools, Synge street, Dublin | × | × | 57 | × | 159 |
| 3840 | Kavanagh, Patrick J., Christian Schools, Limerick | × | × | 405 | × | 311 |
| 3841 | [Not Examined] | × | × | × | × | × |
| 3842 | [Failed] | × | × | f | × | 238 |
| 3843 | Kavanagh, William, Rockwell College, Cashel | × | 608 | 300 | 100 | 336 |
| 3844 | Kealy, Michael, Christian Schools, Gorey | × | f | P | f | 207 |
| 3845 | [Failed] | × | f | f | × | f |
| 3846 | Kean, William F., Christian Schools, Newry | × | × | 410 | × | 285 |
| 3847 | Keane, Daniel, Christian Schools, Newry | × | × | 400 | × | 328 |
| 3848 | [Failed] | × | × | f | × | f |
| 3849 | Keane, William, Christian Schools, Limerick | × | × | 27 | × | 227 |
| 3850 | Keany, Matthew J., St. Patrick's College, Cavan | 38 | 408 | 225 | × | 43 |
| 3851 | [Failed] | × | f | 62 | × | 26 |
| 3852 | Kearney, John, Presentation College, Mardyke, Cork | × | 522 | 275 | 10 | 238 |
| 3853 | [Failed] | × | × | f | × | f |
| 3854 | [Failed] | × | × | f | × | f |
| 3855 | [Failed] | × | f | 95 | × | 75 |
| 3856 | [Failed] | × | × | f | × | f |
| 3857 | [Failed] | × | × | 190 | × | f |
| 3858 | Keeffe, Michael, Christian Schools, New Ross | × | × | 10 | 5 | 68 |
| 3859 | Keeffe, Patrick, Presentation College, Mardyke, Cork | × | × | 110 | × | 132 |
| 3860 | Keeffe, Thomas, St. Munchin's College, Limerick | 381 | 188 | 52 | × | 233 |

Joyce's Intermediate results, 1895.

| Commercial French | German | Commercial German | Italian | Commercial Italian | Spanish | Commercial Spanish | Celtic | Arithmetic | Book-keeping | Euclid | Algebra | Natural Philosophy | Chemistry | Drawing | Shorthand | Total under Rule 55 | Examination Number |
|---|---|---|---|---|---|---|---|---|---|---|---|---|---|---|---|---|---|
| 200 | 700 | 200 | 500 | 200 | 500 | 200 | 600 | 500 | 200 | 600 | 600 | 500 | 500 | 500 | 300 | | |
| x | x | x | x | x | x | x | x | 310 | x | 185 | 150 | x | x | 120 | 190 | 2022 | 3821 |
| x | x | x | x | x | x | x | f | f | x | f | f | x | x | 80 | x | 90 | 3822 |
| 106 | x | x | x | x | x | x | x | 330 | x | 220 | 10 | 130 | 50 | 170 | x | 1859 | 3823 |
| x | x | x | x | x | x | x | x | 10 | x | 165 | 5 | x | x | f | x | 1092 | 3824 |
| x | x | x | x | x | x | x | x | 175 | x | 350 | 275 | x | x | 35 | x | 1085 | 3825 |
| x | x | x | x | x | x | x | x | 20 | P | f | x | x | x | 85 | x | 155 | 3826 |
| x | x | x | x | x | x | x | x | 145 | x | 245 | 30 | f | x | 25 | x | 466 | 3827 |
| x | 92 | x | 94 | x | x | x | 142 | 150 | x | 165 | 60 | 100 | 60 | 135 | x | 1442 | 3828 |
| x | x | x | 223 | x | x | x | x | 250 | x | 175 | 175 | 190 | 100 | x | x | 2699 | 3829 |
| x | x | x | x | x | x | x | x | f | 15 | f | f | x | x | x | x | 42 | 3830 |
| x | x | x | x | x | x | x | x | 205 | f | 50 | f | x | x | 55 | f | 325 | 3831 |
| x | x | x | x | x | x | x | x | f | x | 135 | x | x | x | x | x | 160 | 3832 |
| x | x | x | x | x | x | x | x | 10 | x | 105 | f | x | x | x | x | 352 | 3833 |
| x | x | x | x | x | x | x | x | 110 | x | 155 | f | x | x | x | x | 720 | 3834 |
| x | x | x | x | x | x | x | f | 55 | x | 85 | x | x | x | 160 | x | 1136 | 3835 |
| x | x | x | x | x | x | x | x | f | x | f | f | x | x | f | x | x | 3836 |
| 12 | x | x | x | x | x | x | x | 190 | 50 | 145 | 125 | x | x | 65 | x | 1512 | 3837 |
| f | x | x | x | x | x | x | x | 140 | 10 | 120 | 130 | P | f | f | x | 684 | 3838 |
| x | x | x | x | x | x | x | x | 5 | 40 | 10 | x | x | x | 5 | x | 276 | 3839 |
| x | x | x | x | x | x | x | x | 155 | 85 | 125 | x | x | x | 170 | 25 | 1276 | 3840 |
| x | x | x | x | x | x | x | x | x | x | x | x | x | x | x | x | x | 3841 |
| x | x | x | x | x | x | x | x | f | x | f | x | x | x | 15 | x | 253 | 3842 |
| 106 | 136 | x | 230 | x | x | x | x | 20 | 35 | 165 | 15 | x | x | x | x | 2051 | 3843 |
| 68 | x | x | x | x | x | x | x | 5 | 55 | f | f | x | x | x | 30 | 365 | 3844 |
| x | x | x | x | x | x | x | x | 5 | x | f | f | x | x | x | x | 5 | 3845 |
| x | 157 | x | 167 | x | x | x | 166 | 410 | x | 185 | 115 | 210 | 115 | 115 | x | 2335 | 3846 |
| x | 281 | x | 168 | x | x | x | 322 | 310 | x | 430 | 100 | 250 | 400 | 185 | x | 3174 | 3847 |
| x | x | x | x | x | x | x | x | f | x | f | x | x | x | f | f | x | 3848 |
| x | x | x | x | x | x | x | x | 155 | x | 40 | x | x | x | 30 | x | 479 | 3849 |
| x | x | x | x | x | x | x | x | f | x | 15 | f | 45 | x | f | x | 774 | 3850 |
| x | x | x | x | x | x | x | x | f | x | f | 15 | x | x | x | x | 103 | 3851 |
| 34 | 251 | 1 | 168 | x | x | x | x | 360 | 130 | x | 150 | x | x | 140 | x | 2279 | 3852 |
| x | x | x | x | x | x | x | x | 220 | x | 65 | f | x | x | 105 | x | 390 | 3853 |
| x | x | x | x | x | x | x | x | f | x | x | x | x | x | 35 | x | 35 | 3854 |
| x | x | x | x | x | x | x | x | 5 | x | f | f | x | x | x | x | 175 | 3855 |
| x | x | x | x | x | x | x | x | P | x | 60 | x | x | x | f | x | 60 | 3856 |
| x | x | x | x | x | x | x | x | f | x | f | x | x | x | f | x | 190 | 3857 |
| f | x | x | x | x | x | x | 45 | f | f | 35 | f | 30 | x | 30 | x | 223 | 3858 |
| x | x | x | x | x | x | x | x | 190 | x | 135 | f | x | x | x | x | 567 | 3859 |
| x | x | x | x | x | x | x | x | 15 | x | 75 | f | x | x | x | x | 944 | 3860 |

K

117

offering a place in their college at Newbridge. But Joyce, left to make the decision himself, chose to persevere with the Jesuits.[138]

The summer brought the usual staff changes. Mr McCluskey left and Mr Ryan became Fr Ryan. There were two familiar faces in the Jesuit community when Joyce returned to school. Mr James Jeffcoat and Mr John Gwynne, who had both been in Clongowes when he was there, had come to teach in Belvedere. J. F. Byrne, Cosgrave and Vincent Connolly had left and gone to UCD.[139] Connolly, the one of these whom Joyce seems to have known best at school, transferred to Trinity after a year and later went on to Oxford.[140] But the other two were still in UCD when Joyce went there in 1898 and it was probably only then that he and they really became friends.

On Saturday 7 December 1895 he was received into the Sodality of the Blessed Virgin Mary, along with twenty-one other boys.[141] The procedure would have been familiar enough to him from Clongowes, where he had witnessed sodality receptions on at least three occasions. Fr Cullen, who had revived this sodality in Belvedere, also founded sodalities for the more junior boys.[142] One of these, the Sodality of the Holy Angels, under the direction of Fr Hugh Tunney, was active in the college throughout Joyce's time.[143] It was the ordinary prelude to membership of the senior sodality and it seems safe to presume that Joyce had been a member, quite likely an official. In 1895 the director of the Sodality of the Blessed Virgin was Fr Richard Campbell. He was succeeded in 1896 by Fr Joseph McDonnell, a newcomer to the community. Joyce seems to have intended reference to him in *Stephen Hero* as 'Fr MacNally', but the plan did not survive into *A Portrait*.[144]

Some years after Joyce had been a sodalist, *The Belvederian* contained an account of the sodality which was almost certainly written by Fr McDonnell.[145] It expresses the character and function of the sodality, as seen by the college:

> It is manifest that a select body of boys, chosen by the votes of their companions and superiors, and formed into an association for the purpose of showing special honour to the Virgin Mother of God must, if it were only by the force of their example, exercise a powerful influence for good in any college. . . . The very existence of such an association is a perpetual incentive to piety. Its members are the leading boys, whose position in the house causes them, in some degree, to be looked up to by the younger pupils of the school.

Preparation for life after school was one of the sodality's principal aims:

> It is obvious that the banding together of young men devoted to the pursuit of high ideals, to the safeguarding of Christian faith and

The college chapel at Belvedere, with the statue of the Blessed Virgin Mary on the left. In front of this, Joyce had 'a cushioned kneelingdesk . . . from which he led his wing of boys through the responses at meetings of the sodality' (photograph taken in 1906).

purity of morals, at a time when the temptations of youth and the fascinations of the world appear to be most powerful, can and must be productive of impressions which will last for life.

The final paragraph expressed the purpose not only of the sodality but of the school as a whole:

That all our boys, when they leave us to enter on the race of life, and our Sodalists in particular, may have learned to comport themselves at all times as becomes true Catholic gentlemen, true children of the Church and of their heavenly Mother Mary, is the principal object of their school training and its best result.

It was of such a society in Belvedere that Joyce, at the tender age of thirteen, had now been elected a member. In the light of his later development, this account of the sodality's ideals has considerable dramatic irony. Stephen Dedalus heard about him 'the constant voice

119

of his father and of his masters, urging him to be a gentleman above all things and urging him to be a good catholic above all things' (332–33). If these voices spoke to Joyce, the Jesuits – if not his father – were to be disappointed.

The sodality did not make heavy demands on its members' time. At the weekly meeting on Saturday mornings at 9 a.m., they listened to 'an extract from the history of the Sodality as given in the "Sodality Manual", or some of the rules of the Sodality or a chapter of the "Imitation of Christ" or a passage from some other spiritual book selected by the Director'. This was read by the prefect of the sodality, who then led the others in a recitation of Matins and Lauds of the 'Little Office' of Our Lady. At 9.30 the sodalists attended the school Mass, which two of them served.[146] Apart from that, the demands made by the sodality were in the domain of moral behaviour, not external religious practice. For James Joyce, living only ten minutes away from the school in North Richmond St, the inconvenience of leaving home earlier on Saturday would have been slight. It may have increased when he was in Senior Grade and the family was living in Fairview. In his first year in the sodality, in any case, he had a little more time to spare than before. Since he was under age for Middle Grade,[147] he had no public exam to prepare for in June.

William Fogarty, a lay-master who came to Belvedere in 1909 and later recorded his first impressions of the school, remarked how 'the amount of freedom allowed to the pupils outside the classrooms – an invaluable foretaste of a world in which they would have only their own sense of honour to rely on – came as a shock to one trained on the Continent, where the boys are never trusted out of sight of a teacher, or, at least, of an usher'.[148] It may have been the greater freedom which he enjoyed, combined with the pressures of a precocious sexuality, which now impelled Joyce's 'wanderings' on those 'veiled autumnal evenings' towards the 'narrow and dirty streets' and 'foul laneways' of Dublin (350–51).[149] Home and school were not much more than a stone's throw from the notorious prostitution district of the 'Monto' and the squalor of its adjoining streets.[150] Whatever Joyce may have been doing in his spare time, the rector's suspicions were aroused. According to Stanislaus, he himself was interrogated about James's behaviour and both parents were subsequently warned in vague terms about their eldest son.[151]

Whatever Fr Henry's misgivings about him, Joyce was made prefect of the sodality on 25 September 1896, shortly after coming back to begin his second-last year in school. He was then little more than fourteen-and-a-half. Albrecht Connolly became first assistant prefect, elected, like Joyce, by the votes of the other members of the sodality.[152] It was now Joyce's responsibility to read at the beginning

120

Belvedere College as seen from North Great George's St. The bottom of this street was not far from Joyce's 'Nighttown' (photograph taken about 1910).

of sodality meetings and, like Stephen, from 'his cushioned kneeling-desk at the right of the altar' in the Boys' Chapel, to lead the responses for his side in the 'Little Office' (356). The significance of his election extended far beyond such minor functions within the sodality. In the absence of boy-prefects or organised teamgames, the sodality election was the only means of identifying leadership quality among the boys. Joyce and Connolly, as a result of their election, were 'virtual heads of the school' and 'it was they who went up to the rector together to ask for a free day or to get a fellow off' (324). It was, no doubt, an unflattering reflection on the 'undistinguished dullards' in Senior Grade that these responsibilities had been entrusted to two of their juniors (Connolly and Joyce were now in Middle Grade). But it was also a striking tribute to the standing both of them, and Joyce in particular, enjoyed among their contemporaries.[153]

Albrecht Connolly was to remain faithful to the sodality for the rest of his short life. Having attended UCD with Joyce in 1898,[154] he later went out to Mexico to become Instructor in Musketry to the War Office there. He caught yellow fever and died after five days, on 23 September 1908, before taking up the position. The nuns in whose care he spent his last hours sent home an account of his death, which the annual of his old school was proud to publish:

He asked for and got an English-speaking priest from whom he

121

received the Last Sacraments, and to whom he showed the Cross of the B.V.M. Sodality which had been pinned to his breast in Belvedere some ten years before. He had treasured it through all his wanderings, and never ceased to wear it wherever he went.[155]

Stephen had proudly hung up the illuminated scroll which certified his prefecture of the sodality on his bedroom wall. But even at the time he knew 'the falsehood of his position' (356). The end of November brought the annual retreat, in preparation for the feast of the college patron St Francis Xavier on 3 December, and the full anomaly of Joyce's situation was revealed to him.[156]

He would have been familiar with retreats from his days in Clongowes, where they took place each year in September. He may not have followed the retreat exercises, at least in the earlier years, but he would certainly have done so since coming to Belvedere. The retreats followed a familiar pattern based on the 'First Week' of the *Spiritual Exercises* of St Ignatius.[157] The retreat of 1896 was memorable less for what was actually said than for the spiritual crisis it not surprisingly precipitated in the only retreatant of that year who has left us a record of it. Vincent Heron could chat equably enough about the 'blue funk' they had all been put in by the morning sermon they had just heard on the pains of hell (380), and Mr Tate could rib him on the salutary effect this might be expected to have on their work. Both of them probably forgot it soon enough. For Stephen (and Joyce), such detachment was impossible. It merely served to heighten the feeling of isolation and moral degradation.

Joyce's use of the name 'Fr Arnall' for the preacher of the retreat is purely symbolic.[158] The Clongowes 'Fr Arnall' was Fr William Power. There is no possibility that he gave the retreat. School retreats were never given in one college by Jesuit teachers from another: their work would not permit it.[159] Moreover, Fr Power would not at that time have been entrusted with the delicate task of conducting a schoolboys' retreat.[160] The 'tradition among Irish Jesuits' quoted by Sullivan that the retreat director was in fact Fr James A. Cullen seems entirely sound.[161] It is accepted by Ellmann, who corroborates it with evidence from Thomas Bodkin.[162] The latter, who was on the Belvedere rolls a little after James Joyce, rightly emphasises the detail of the preacher's 'heavy cloak': this was very unusual for a Jesuit but Fr Cullen did wear one. (It may have been a relic of his days as a secular priest, before becoming a Jesuit.) It is a detail which was also remembered by another pupil from this period, writing general reminiscences of his schooldays in *The Belvederian* in 1929. Jack Burke-Gaffney, slightly younger than Thomas Bodkin, recalled 'Father Cullen with his head on one side and his cloak over his shoulders, a

Fr James Cullen S.J., the probable preacher of the 1896 retreat in Belvedere.

little bit of the chain which should fasten it always dangling at the collar'.[163]

James Cullen was an obvious choice. He had been 'spiritual father' to the boys in Belvedere since 1884,[164] a position which involved no teaching but occasional sermons and private interviews with individuals. In the early years, as we have seen, he had had charge of the BVM sodality but later this office had been transferred to others. He had a number of onerous responsibilities not connected with the school and travelled constantly, hearing confessions and giving sermons, missions and retreats around the country. These included school retreats – he had, for example, given the Clongowes retreat in September 1884.[165] Fr McKenna, his biographer, specifically mentions that he 'gave the annual Boys' retreat for some years' in Belvedere, adding that 'few of those who heard him can forget the impression which he produced'.[166]

Fr Cullen was a remarkable organiser and an intensely zealous priest. Such a man, with his great capacity to inspire others, ought to have been optimistic in outlook himself. Yet, as his biographer remarks, 'in spite of this ever-inspiring enthusiasm, he remained, in his habit of mind, his manner of speech, his voice, his very appearance, a pessimist'.[167] Elsewhere he writes:

> Father Cullen had none of the joyousness of manner which is so often found allied with great sanctity. He was by nature of a melancholy disposition. His face had habitually a rather sad expression, and his tone of voice, even in conversation, but especially when speaking in public, was somewhat funereal.[168]

He was, finally, almost morbidly introspective. He wrote somewhere in his diary: 'I must not depress myself too much by constantly keeping my eyes on the swarming pestilential brood of my faults'.[169] It was this man who actually spoke to the Belvedere boys in 1896.

If the reference in *A Portrait* to 'a heavy cloak' worn by the retreat-giver (361) is a clue to his identity as Fr Cullen, it is not intended to claim that the rest of Joyce's description of 'Fr Arnall' and his retreat is meant to evoke Fr Cullen's image. The writer's clearly symbolic intentions rule this out. When we turn to the matter of the retreat itself, it is even more important to keep in mind the distinction between the character of Joyce's historical experience and the literary sources on which he drew in his novel in order to represent that experience in fictional terms.

The retreat, as Joyce reports it, begins with an instruction on Wednesday afternoon and ends with Mass on Saturday morning. This seems to correspond to the procedure actually followed. Unlike Clongowes, where class was suspended and the retreat exercises extended throughout the entire day, the Belvedere retreat-order was superimposed on the ordinary timetable and ended at three o'clock, as school usually did. In this arrangement, two of the four daily classes survived, one in the morning and one in the afternoon. A few years later, at least, there were three instructions each day – one after morning Mass, one before lunch and following recitation of beads, and finally one after the afternoon class, before the boys went home.[170] This was probably the order in Joyce's time too. According to Fr McKenna, it had been one of the spontaneous effects of Fr Cullen's earliest retreats in Belvedere that 'at the end of the school-day the boys, instead of going home as was their custom in groups of twos and threes, went home singly and in silence'.[171] From Joyce's description, the custom was still alive in 1896 and the boys observed silence during the retreat, apart from class-time.[172] He quotes the entire introductory sermon, given on Wednesday afternoon, summarises the Thursday sermons on 'death and judgment' and quotes at great length both of the sermons given on Friday.[173]

J. R. Thrane has clearly demonstrated that, to compose his two sermons on hell, Joyce used the seventeenth-century Jesuit Giovanni Pietro Pinamonti's tract *Hell Opened to Christians, To Caution Them from Entering It*, a translation of which was published by James Duffy in 1868.[174] Thrane argues that Joyce was familiar with the late Victorian debate about hell. He knew the Redemptorist John Joseph Furniss's terrific *The Sight of Hell* with its crude, materialistic representations of hell-fire, and the sinister Italian work by Pinamonti which is possibly its source. So much for what Joyce knew. With regard to Fr Cullen, Thrane knows of 'no evidence that he ever employed either of the two tracts in describing the punishment of sin'.[175] What did Fr Cullen employ? He kept very copious diaries, on which his biographer Fr McKenna was able to draw extensively,[176] but these have disappeared. One book, however, has survived which is worth closer examination in the present context.

This is called *Instructions for Youth in Christian Piety Taken from the Sacred Scriptures, and the Writings of the Holy Fathers* by the Rev. Charles Gobinet, D.D. A new edition, in translation from the French, was published by James Duffy one year before his edition of Pinamonti, in 1867.[177] The book, which contains two volumes in one, has predictable contents. Volume one treats of the reasons and motives which oblige men to apply themselves to virtue in their youth (part 1), the necessary means of acquiring virtue during youth (2), the obstacles which withdraw young persons from virtue (3), the virtues necessary for young persons (4), and the choice of a state of life (5). Volume two, which is almost half of the book,[178] contains an exhortation to engage young persons to return to God, by penance, and a serious amendment of life (part 6) and goes on to treat of contrition (7), confession (8), satisfaction (9) and the preservation of grace after confession, against a relapse into sin (10). This volume closes with instructions concerning Holy Communion and there is a supplement containing instructions on prayer. In his lengthy treatment of repentance and confession, Gobinet devotes an extended chapter to 'the dreadful effects of mortal sin' and considers in particular 'the effects of sin in hell'.[179] None of this makes his book remarkable or of any special interest in relation to Joyce. As Thrane recognises, the considerations to be found in Fr Arnall's sermons were a commonplace of preaching and spiritual writing in that period. Gobinet, with his conviction that 'hell is daily filled with millions of souls, and few, very few, enter into heaven in comparison',[180] belongs to the tradition current in Joyce's day and stretching back to Pinamonti in the seventeenth century and beyond.

What makes Gobinet more interesting than a host of other volumes of a similar kind is the simple fact that Fr James Cullen possessed a copy all through his years as spiritual father in Belvedere (1883–1904), recommended it for reading to the members of his sodality in the school[181] and used it himself for sermons and retreats. A copy of the book has survived in Belvedere bearing his signature: 'Rev. J. A. Cullen S.J., Belvedere College S.J., Dublin 26/2/1885'. The inside front cover contains, in his hand, a detailed index of subjects and illustrations treated in Gobinet with the number of the relevant page, collected with a view to use in preaching. Throughout the book, words are underlined and the margins are filled with summaries, cross-references and the mnemonics which he was accustomed to use in his diaries.[182] In the diaries such codes were in aid of his own progress; in Gobinet they were a guide to his preaching to young people. Fr Cullen had been at school in Clongowes himself but, when he felt a call to the priesthood, he had decided against joining the Jesuits because, above all, he disliked the prospect of teaching.[183] Within a few months of being appointed to Belvedere and given responsibility for the spiritual welfare of the boys, he obtained a copy of Gobinet. Gobinet had actually written the book in similar circumstances.[184] When he was transferred to Gardiner St in 1904, to work more exclusively with adults, he left *Instructions for Youth in Christian Piety* to his successor in Belvedere.

Gobinet's treatment of hell begins with an invitation to the reader: 'Let us go down into the pit of hell, that so we may conceive a more lively apprehension of the enormity of mortal sin'.[185] From this he will learn firstly to detest sin, secondly to fear 'that abyss of misery to which sin exposes us'.[186] The author quotes the traditional catechism definition of hell as 'an eternal fire, which God has prepared for the devil and his apostate angels, and with which he has also decreed to punish the sins of men, who follow the rebellious example of those ambitious spirits'. He bases the definition on Matthew 25,41: 'Depart from me, ye cursed, into everlasting fire, which was prepared for the devil and his angels', in which he discovers the four elements of which hell's punishment is composed. These are 'the separation from God, the curse of God, fire, and eternity'.[187] He develops each of these points in turn and ends with a series of reflections: the inadequacy of words to describe the reality of hell, the justice of this punishment, the fact that our sins have merited such retribution, that God's goodness alone had thus far preserved us from it, that without repentance we cannot avoid it.[188]

It will be immediately apparent how widely Gobinet's treatment differs in its structure and presentation from that of the preacher in *A Portrait*. It is possible to find points of similarity in detail, as the following examples suggest:

| | |
|---|---|
| . . . if one were constrained to put his finger into the fire but for a quarter of an hour, it could not be endured (Gobinet, p. 324). | Place your finger for a moment in the flame of a candle and you will feel the pain of fire (*A Portrait* p. 375). |
| This fire, by another extraordinary quality, burns all without either consuming the subject upon which it acts, or even spending its own substance. Our fire consumes the things it burns, which when it has destroyed, it spends itself for want of fuel; but the fire of hell is of a quite contrary nature, ever burning without consuming, and ever tormenting without diminution or abatement (p. 323). | Our earthly fire also consumes more or less rapidly according as the object which it attacks is more or less combustible so that human ingenuity has even succeeded in inventing chemical preparations to check or frustrate its action. But the sulphurous brimstone which burns in hell is a substance which is specially designed to burn for ever and for ever with an unspeakable fury. Moreover our earthly fire destroys at the same time as it burns so that the more intense it is the shorter is its duration: but the fire of hell has this property that it preserves that which it burns and though it rages with incredible intensity it rages for ever (p. 375–6). |
| Now, for the better escaping this dreadful misfortune, let us consider its duration; which will not be for a day, or a year, or a hundred years, but for all eternity (p. 324). | What must it be, then, to bear the manifold tortures of hell forever? For ever! For all eternity! Not for a year or for an age but for ever (p. 388). |

But the similarity is only approximate and, among commonplaces on the topic of hell, these are the most commonplace of all. The parallels with Pinamonti are much closer. Clearly, Joyce used a literary model to compose his sermons and Pinamonti was at least his principal model. But there is no evidence to show that Fr Cullen, who gave the sermons Joyce the schoolboy actually heard, knew, much less used, Pinamonti. No one has ever suggested that the sermons in *A Portrait* are a detailed reminiscence on Joyce's part of something he once heard. It cannot be proved that Cullen used Gobinet in the Belvedere retreat in 1896. But he is more likely to have done so than to have used Pinamonti. He certainly used it on other occasions and it brings us closer to the mind of the real preacher than the sermons with which Fr Arnall terrorised Stephen Dedalus.[189]

A retreat based on Gobinet would have been a considerably milder affair than Fr Arnall's homiletic fireworks. Despite what seems an excessive stress on the negative side of Christian faith and an absence of any reference in explicit terms to the joys of heaven,[190] Gobinet's purpose is not so much to frighten as to effect genuine conversion. Hell for him is the revelation of what sin is, rather than God's way of terrorising sinners. Fr Cullen, in his earlier years at least, was given to 'hammering' at such topics as 'the punishments of sin' and it is likely that his 'lurid style' heightened the dramatic quality of his material, however sober it may have been.[191] A boy who heard him in Belvedere a few years later wrote that 'his voice was very lugubrious and when he spoke in the chapel he was very solemn'.[192] But 'solemn' and 'lugubrious' are far too mild to characterise the preacher in *A Portrait*. The drama of the 1896 retreat was probably created less by the style or content of the preacher, lurid or dramatic as he may have been, than by the confused state of Joyce's conscience and the extreme ambivalence of his position.[193]

When Fr Cullen had preached the Clongowes retreat in 1884, the boys flocked to confession afterwards.[194] The reform his retreat of 1896 precipitated in Joyce's life lasted, in Ellmann's estimation, 'some months, probably well into 1897'.[195] Stanislaus speaks of 'the Lenten sermon preached by Father Jeffcott' stirring up a 'brain-storm of terror and remorse' in his brother. This sounds like a reference to the retreat of December 1896.[196] If so, the preacher was Cullen, not 'Jeffcott'.[197] Mr James Jeffcoat was not, in any case, ordained until 1899. It is possible that Joyce had contact with him at this period, as Stanislaus suggests. He had been taught by Jeffcoat in Clongowes and they would have met again in Belvedere the previous year when Jeffcoat was a scholastic in the community. It is also possible that he was in touch with Fr Conmee in Gardiner St. But Stanislaus is never reliable on such details.[198]

Whatever moral or religious crisis Joyce experienced at the end of 1896, it does not seem to have led to any neglect of his studies. Perhaps it actually helped. His results in the Middle Grade examination that summer were the best he achieved during his school career. Apart from English, his marks were up in all subjects (including mathematics), when compared with the Junior Grade results of two years before.[199] In Latin, this was the year when he had studied Book VIII of Ovid's *Metamorphoses* and read, perhaps for the first time, the story of Daedalus.[200] It was from this book that he was to take the motto which he prefixed to *A Portrait*: 'et ignotas animun dimittit in artes' (I.188). The account of how Daedalus constructed wings for himself and his son Icarus (II.183ff) did not come up in the examination, but a later passage involving Daedalus was asked about: his performance of the burial rites of his son (II.244–51). Stephen would recall being taught to construe Ovid by Fr Henry 'in a courtly English, made whimsical by the mention of porkers and potsherds and chines of bacon'. This was also the year when Joyce would have studied 'what little he knew of the laws of Latin verse from a ragged book written by a Portuguese priest' (441), the sixteenth-century Jesuit grammarian Manoel Alvarez.[201] In the Middle Grade, apart from scanning Ovid, students were expected to compose Latin verse. The other set text was Cicero's *de Senectute*. The Roman history course went down as far as Marius and Sulla. There were elements in the Latin syllabus for 1897 which Joyce certainly remembered. Although he never again reached 700, his mark in Preparatory Grade, his Latin improved slightly to 642.

His marks in French (where he read de Witt's *Derrière les haies* and Coppée's *Le luthier de Crémone*) were the best he achieved in the four years of the Intermediate: 528 out of 700, a very creditable performance. His Italian marks (342 out of 500) were also his best ever.[202] Only English was down, back to the level he had reached in Preparatory Grade. The prescribed authors were Milton (*Lycidas, Il Penseroso* and *L'Allegro*), Gray (*Elegy, The Bard, Ode on Eton College*) and Goldsmith (*Selected Essays*). The second paper, which contained Goldsmith as well as the usual history (down to 1714) and geography questions, also had a section entitled 'Outlines of English Literature from Chaucer to Milton, both inclusive'. Joyce probably picked up the bulk of his marks in the composition (for which 250 were available). The titles were:

(a) Describe the plot of any work of fiction you have read.
(b) 'Ye gentlemen of England that live at home in ease,
　　Ah! little do ye think upon the dangers of the seas'.
(c) 'Gay Hope is theirs by Fancy fed,
　　Less pleasing when possest'.

(Gray: *Ode on Eton College*).

| Examination Number | STUDENT'S NAME AND ADDRESS | Greek | Latin | English | Commercial English | French | Commercial French |
|---|---|---|---|---|---|---|---|
| | MAXIMUM .. | 1200 | 1200 | 1200 | 400 | 700 | 200 |
| 6141 | Herlihy,. Daniel J., St. Brendan's Seminary, Killarney [**J.Ex.**'96] | 450 | 392 | 221 | x | 470 | x |
| 6142 | [Failed] | x | 16 | f | x | 307 | x |
| 6143 | Hickman, Poole H., Grammar School. Tipperary [**J.Ex.**'96] | 97 | 303 | 134 | x | 384 | x |
| 6144 | Higgins, Daniel J., St. Patrick's Seminary, Bruff | 25 | 84 | 10 | x | 349 | x |
| 6145 | [Failed] | x | 7 | f | x | 223 | x |
| 6146 | [Failed] | f | f | f | x | 321 | x |
| 6147 | [Failed] | x | 10 | f | x | 200 | x |
| 6148 | Horgan, David, Christian Schools, Cork [**J.Ex.**'96] | x | 424 | 40 | x | 366 | 36 |
| 6149 | [Failed] | x | f | f | x | 67 | x |
| 6150 | Horgan, Michael, St. Brendan's Seminary, Killarney [**J.Ex.**'96] | 250 | 331 | 72 | x | 309 | x |
| 6151 | Horgan, Michael J., Christian Schools, Cork [**J.Ex.**'96] | x. | 441 | 153 | x | 358 | x |
| 6152 | Houghton, Kenneth A. H., Corrig School, Kingstown [**J.Ex.**'96] | x | 268 | 233 | x | 366 | x |
| 6153 | Houston, Joseph W., Academical Institution Coleraine | 62 | 48 | 226 | x | 179 | x |
| 6154 | [Failed] | f | 294 | f | x | 249 | x |
| 6155 | Hughes, James J., Christian Schools, N. Richmond street, Dublin | x | 557 | 226 | x | 460 | 31 |
| 6156 | [Not Examined] | x | x | x | x | x | x |
| 6157 | Hurley, Timothy, St. Colman's College, Fermoy [**J.Ex.**'96] | 580 | 565 | 308 | x | 398 | x |
| 6158 | Hynes, Michael. Christian Schools, Mullingar | x | 118 | 144 | x | 237 | f |
| 6159 | [Failed] | x | f | f | x | 24 | x |
| 6160 | Irvine, James P., Grammar School, Larne | x | f | 105 | x | 55 | x |
| 6161 | Irwin, David, Foyle College, Londonderry [**J.Ex.**'96] | x | 241 | 129 | x | 337 | x |
| 6162 | Irwin, William, St. Patrick's Seminary, Bruff [**J.Ex.**'96] | 425 | 530 | 179 | x | 530 | x |
| 6163 | [Failed] | x | f | f | x | 215 | x |
| 6164 | [Failed] | x | x | f | x | 100 | x |
| 6165 | [Failed] | x | f | f | x | f | f |
| 6166 | Jackson, Thomas, Royal Academical Institution, Belfast | x | x | 30 | x | 297 | x |
| 6167 | [Failed] | f | f | f | x | 104 | x |
| 6168 | Johnston, John, Royal School, Dungannon [**J.Ex.**'96] | 515 | 471 | 222 | x | 392 | x |
| 6169 | Johnston, Samuel A., Royal School, Dungannon | x | 135 | 81 | x | 277 | x |
| 6170 | Johnston, William J. McM., Royal Academical Institution, Belfast | x | 7 | 34 | 70 | 259 | x |
| 6171 | Jones, Christopher F., High School, Dublin [**J.Ex.**'96] | x | 471 | 274 | 105 | 388 | 28 |
| 6172 | [Failed] | x | 201 | f | x | 152 | x |
| 6173 | [Failed] | x | x | f | x | 229 | f |
| 6174 | Joyce, James A., Belvedere College (s.J.), Dublin | x | 642 | 457 | x | 528 | 33 |
| 6175 | [Failed] | x | x | f | x | f | x |
| 6176 | [Failed] | x | f | f | x | 354 | x |
| 6177 | [Failed] | 7 | f | f | x | 248 | x |
| 6178 | [Failed] | x | f | f | x | 48 | x |
| 6179 | [Failed] | x | f | f | x | f | x |
| 6180 | Keeffe, Thomas, St. Munchin's College, Limerick | f | 187 | 11 | x | 414 | x |

Joyce's Intermediate results, 1897.

| German 700 | Commercial German 200 | Italian 500 | Commercial Italian 200 | Spanish 500 | Commercial Spanish 200 | Celtic 600 | Arithmetic 500 | Book-keeping 200 | Euclid 600 | Algebra 600 | Natural Philosophy 500 | Chemistry 500 | Drawing 500 | Shorthand 300 | Precis Writing 200 | Total under Rule 56 | Examination Number |
|---|---|---|---|---|---|---|---|---|---|---|---|---|---|---|---|---|---|
| × | × | × | × | × | × | × | 135 | × | 175 | 70 | × | × | × | × | × | 1913 | 6141 |
| × | × | × | × | × | × | × | f | × | 30 | 10 | × | × | × | × | × | 363 | 6142 |
| × | × | × | × | × | × | × | 330 | × | 460 | 370 | × | × | × | × | × | 2078 | 6143 |
| × | × | × | × | × | × | × | f | × | 15 | f | × | × | × | × | × | 483 | 6144 |
| × | × | × | × | × | × | × | 45 | × | 10 | f | × | × | × | × | × | 285 | 6145 |
| × | × | × | × | × | × | × | 75 | × | 130 | 50 | × | × | × | × | × | 576 | 6146 |
| × | × | × | × | × | × | × | 60 | × | 65 | f | × | × | × | × | × | 335 | 6147 |
| × | × | × | × | × | × | 266 | 10 | 40 | 70 | × | 45 | × | × | 44 | × | 1341 | 6148 |
| × | × | × | × | × | × | × | 195 | × | 50 | 100 | × | × | × | × | × | 412 | 6149 |
| y | × | × | × | × | × | × | 220 | × | 105 | 35 | × | × | × | × | × | 1322 | 6150 |
| z | × | × | × | × | × | 250 | 105 | 140 | 175 | f | × | × | × | 192 | × | 1814 | 6151 |
| 232 | × | × | ● | × | × | × | 205 | × | 170 | × | 40 | × | × | × | × | 1514 | 6152 |
| × | × | × | × | × | × | × | f | × | P | f | × | × | × | × | × | 515 | 6153 |
| × | × | × | × | × | × | × | f | × | 75 | f | × | × | × | × | × | 618 | 6154 |
| 428 | × | × | × | × | × | 245 | 115 | × | × | 195 | × | × | × | × | 65 | 2322 | 6155 |
| × | × | × | × | × | × | × | × | × | × | × | × | × | × | × | × | × | 6156 |
| × | × | 208 | × | × | × | × | 210 | × | × | 330 | × | × | × | × | × | 2599 | 6157 |
| × | × | × | × | × | × | × | 140 | × | 95 | P | × | × | × | × | × | 734 | 6158 |
| × | × | × | × | × | × | × | f | × | 105 | f | f | × | 50 | × | × | 179 | 6159 |
| × | × | × | × | × | × | × | 85 | 10 | 150 | f | 75 | × | f | × | × | 480 | 6160 |
| × | × | × | × | × | × | × | 500 | 120 | 490 | 480 | 245 | 224 | × | × | × | 2766 | 6161 |
| × | × | × | × | × | × | × | 225 | × | 190 | 145 | × | × | × | × | × | 2224 | 6162 |
| × | × | × | × | × | × | × | f | × | f | f | × | × | f | f | × | 215 | 6163 |
| 279 | × | × | × | × | × | × | 105 | × | 40 | 65 | × | × | × | × | × | 589 | 6164 |
| × | × | × | × | × | × | × | f | × | f | f | f | f | × | × | × | × | 6165 |
| × | × | × | × | × | × | × | 55 | × | 95 | P | × | × | × | × | × | 477 | 6166 |
| × | × | × | × | × | × | × | f | × | f | × | × | × | P | × | × | 104 | 6167 |
| × | × | × | × | × | × | × | 260 | × | 275 | 220 | × | × | × | × | × | 2355 | 6168 |
| × | × | × | × | × | × | × | 30 | × | 130 | f | × | × | × | × | × | 653 | 6169 |
| × | × | × | × | × | × | × | 5 | × | f | × | 55 | × | × | × | 60 | 490 | 6170 |
| × | × | × | × | × | × | × | 440 | × | 190 | 360 | × | × | × | 123 | 90 | 2469 | 6171 |
| × | × | × | × | × | × | × | 50 | 70 | 210 | 55 | × | × | 55 | × | × | 793 | 6172 |
| × | × | × | × | × | × | 122 | 250 | × | 145 | 360 | 80 | 125 | f | × | × | 1311 | 6173 |
| × | × | 342 | × | × | × | × | 340 | × | 180 | 230 | 175 | × | × | f | × | 2927 | 6174 |
| × | × | × | × | × | × | × | f | × | f | × | × | × | f | × | × | × | 6175 |
| × | × | × | × | × | × | × | 20 | × | 145 | f | × | × | × | × | × | 519 | 6176 |
| × | × | × | × | × | × | × | f | × | 160 | f | × | × | × | × | × | 415 | 6177 |
| × | × | × | × | × | × | × | f | × | 15 | × | × | × | × | × | × | 63 | 6178 |
| × | × | × | × | × | × | × | 5 | × | 55 | f | × | × | × | × | × | 60 | 6179 |
| × | × | × | × | × | × | × | 110 | × | 140 | f | × | × | × | × | × | 862 | 6180 |

131

Joyce won a £3 prize for the best composition in Middle Grade. As the essay he wrote on a previous occasion for George Dempsey on the topic 'Trust not appearances' shows well enough, he was quite capable of composing in the sententious style invited by the second and third titles above.[203] But it seems much more likely that his prize-winning essay was written on the first title. This was the period when, according to Ellmann, 'he read a great many books of all kinds at high speed', in particular the novels of Meredith and Hardy.[204] It is extremely improbable that many other Middle Grade candidates in 1897 were remotely as well read as he was. He could hardly have asked for a more ideal topic to write on, if he had been given the choice himself.

Although he had one subject less than in Junior Grade (having dropped chemistry as a useless encumbrance),[205] he still managed to come thirteenth out of thirty-four exhibitioners and was awarded £30, tenable for three years, to go with his English prize. By dint of the latter, he joined a long line of George Dempsey's pupils who won distinctions over the years. In 1910, when Dempsey's silver jubilee on the Belvedere staff was being celebrated, a list of these pupils (up to date) was published in the school magazine.[206] Apart from C. Dawson, C. J. McGarry, V. A. Cox and A. C. J. Cox, who won medals in English, the following were awarded prizes in English composition: E. H. Cannon, J. E. Stoer,[207] R. L. Keegan, J. Doran, W. Dawson, C. J. Sullivan, P. J. Murray, C. Coppinger, R. Sheehy, J. A. Joyce (2), J. J. Headen, B. Gibney, E. Sheehy, M. Drummond, V A. Cox (3), A. C. J. Cox (4) and E. T. Freeman (2). This makes a remarkable total of twenty-four prizes in twenty-five years. Joyce's achievement was not unique, but he was keeping distinguished company.

When he returned to school in September 1897, his position as unofficial head-boy of Belvedere was impregnable. He was duly re-elected prefect of the sodality in December.[208] By now, well into 1897,[209] the effects of the previous year's retreat were wearing off, even if he did not fully abandon the practice of religion until somewhat later. There is no indication that his final school retreat (about which we know nothing) had any comparable impact to the one Fr Cullen had preached in 1896. The scruples of conscience which had caused him such anguish then would not be allowed to trouble him again. Once he had disowned these scruples, he took care to distance himself from those whom he blamed for implanting them in him in the first place. Proof against serious sanction or even disapprobation by virtue of his position as sodality prefect and his academic distinction, he was free to behave with studied aloofness towards the school authorities. If Fr Henry, the rector and prefect of studies, was the main target of Joyce's feelings of resentment, not even the admired Mr Dempsey escaped. The point is well illustrated in Eugene Sheehy's story about Joyce's unpunctuality for English class and his impertinent demeanour in reporting himself to Fr Henry.[210] Although still only fifteen-and-a-half, James Joyce had in many respects already left school.

Something of the same attitude emerges in regard to the school gymnasium. This had been established by the new minister of that year, Fr Nicholas J. Tomkin.[211] The theatre had been equipped for the purpose, physical education became part of the school curriculum and a member of the Army Gymnastic Staff, Sergeant-Major Herbert Wright, was entrusted with its supervision.[212] Stephen Dedalus thought of Wright as 'the plump bald sergeantmajor' (321). The Intermediate inspectors who called to Belvedere in October 1901 reported that 'we were shown a fine gymnasium, in which the boys were being drilled by a smart and efficient instructor, and the performances we saw were well executed'.[213] The venture had immediate success: Belvedere won the Schools' Shield of the Irish Amateur Gymnastic Society that year (with Stanislaus Joyce in the team)[214] and for the next four years in succession. 'When the gymnasium had been opened' Stephen Dedalus heard a voice 'urging him to be strong and manly and healthy' (333). Joyce, like Stephen,

The theatre in Belvedere, equipped as a gymnasium (photograph published in *The Belvederian*, 1906).

Sergeant-Major Wright and gymnasts at Belvedere in 1909.

'in deference to his reputation for essay writing . . . had been elected secretary to the gymnasium' (321).[215] Neither took gymnastics very seriously. As Joyce told Gorman afterwards, 'the only thing I could do properly was a half-lever which I could do apparently without muscles till further orders, to the sergeant major's amazement'.[216] In the end, Wright would have to tell him to stop. But the impression of zeal was specious and Joyce was not in earnest. On one occasion he arrived 'all doubled up' and announced to the sergeant-major, 'I've come to be cured'.[217]

Joyce's disaffection, however, was still not public. By reputation he was 'a model youth' (324), and Fr Henry seems to have shared this general estimate of the boy who was captain of the school in all but name. He and Joyce would have had regular personal contacts because of this position and, for him, Joyce would undoubtedly have been the most significant boy in the school. Those who knew William Henry agreed that, despite his outward severity, he had a great affection for the boys in his care, an affection which they returned.[218] Joyce could be infuriating, as the rector knew only too well. But he seems to have had enough restraint (as, in his case, we might expect) not to be put off by this gifted boy's occasional foibles. According to *A Portrait*, the suggestion that Stephen consider a vocation took place in an interview at the beginning of the school year. Stanislaus confirms

The cast of *Vice Versa*, gymnasts and 'Neapolitan peasants' who took part in the Whitsuntide entertainment at Belvedere in 1898. James Joyce is seated in the centre, as Dr Grimstone (wearing mortar-board), with Albrecht Connolly to the right (wearing a top-hat). Stanislaus Joyce is second from the left in the back row, together with Eugene and Richard Sheehy (fifth and sixth from the left, respectively).

that such an interview did take place.[219] It seems probable, however, that discussion on the subject lasted over several weeks or even months and that Joyce did not, in any case, make up his mind quite as quickly as Stephen. The suggestion would have been a natural one to such a boy and there is no need to impute 'jesuit craft' to Fr Henry for making it (415).[220] But if there had ever been a time when Joyce might have been able to follow the suggestion, it was now too late.

Joyce the mimic (like his father before him)[221] was an obvious choice to take part in the Whitsuntide play which Mr Doyle, 'a plump freshfaced jesuit' (333), was getting up. It was to be preceded by a gymnastic display, letting parents see the fruitful results of this new addition to the school curriculum, and some Neapolitan dancing by the small boys. Stanislaus Joyce and the two Sheehys took part in the gym display.[222] The play in 1898[223] was an adaptation of F. Anstey's school-story *Vice Versa*,[224] which, as Ellmann notes, 'dealt farcically with the theme of father against son that Joyce was to use to such good purpose in his later books'.[225] Anstey's novel becomes even more farcical in the simplistic stage-adaptation made by Edward Rose.[226] Mr Bultitude and his son Dick come, magically, to inhabit each other's bodies with the awkward result that the father has to take his son's place at Dr Grimstone's school in the second act. This leads to a predictable variety of misunderstandings, some of which involve Dr Grimstone's rather forward daughter Dulcie. The headmaster, increasingly exasperated at the strange behaviour of the 'boy', is just about to administer a flogging when his 'father' arrives and the day is eventually saved. Afterwards father and son understand one another a little better.

Albrecht Connolly played Bultitude senior and James Joyce the 'farcical pedagogue', Dr Grimstone, a leading role but perhaps not 'the chief part' (321). This character was described in the play as 'a tall, stern, clerical-looking man'. Joyce would have been well cast in such a part. In addition, the incentive to 'take off' Fr Henry must have been strong. According to Eugene Sheehy, Joyce proceeded to disregard his lines and mimic the rector's pet sayings, gestures and mannerisms, 'often for five minutes at a time'. Not surprisingly, the rest of the cast were unable to contain themselves and completely lost their cues. Even Fr Henry, like the rest of the audience, appeared to find the whole thing highly amusing.[227] In *A Portrait*, Stephen's preoccupation is not with Fr Henry but with another member of the audience and how she will react to his performance. He tells us of his humiliation at some of the lines he has to speak. It must be admitted that the thought of that superior, complex adolescent enunciating some of Dr Grimstone's sillier lines is almost embarrassing even now. On the other hand, Joyce may have enjoyed the irony of his position,

Close-up of Joyce and Connolly in the cast of *Vice Versa*.

with the rector and his parents sitting in front of him, as he cried to Connolly: 'Rise unaided, boy; try to stand erect in the presence of the outraged father, and the preceptor of youth whose walls you have sullied too long'. But he may have found it simplest to remove any pretence of taking his role seriously and to render the evening even more farcical than Mr Rose – or Mr Doyle S.J. – had intended.

The day before the Intermediate began, a few weeks later, there was a sudden crisis when Joyce, Connolly and two other boys did not turn up for Fr Henry's catechetical examination. The rector threatened to exclude them from the Intermediate itself; for him, this act of defiance may have been the last straw. Joyce, like Stephen Dedalus, was given to baiting him in catechism class. And now the boy who had feigned interest in the subject during the year did not even bother to sit the examination. In the event, Joyce's French teacher, Mr Andrew McErlean (who had succeeded Fr Ryan in this capacity), intervened and the difficulty was smoothed over.[228]

This incident raises the interesting but unfortunately elusive issue of what exactly Joyce and his contemporaries were taught as religious knowledge. Stephen muses on 'the curious questions' proposed to his mind in the rector's class (358). He ranges over the moral issue of

137

restitution, the proper mode of administering Baptism, the correct understanding of the beatitudes and the theology of the Eucharist. This presumably offers some reflection of the questions touched on in Joyce's own religious knowledge class. In the library in Belvedere, where Fr Cullen's copy of Gobinet was found, there was also a translation of the Belgian Jesuit Fr F. X. Schouppe's *Abridged Course of Religious Instruction, Apologetic, Dogmatic, and Moral: for the Use of Catholic Colleges and Schools,* a 'new edition, thoroughly revised, with the Imprimatur of H. E. Cardinal Manning', published in 1880.[229] The contents of what is really an extended catechism, revised in the wake of the First Vatican Council (1869–70), are summarised in the preface:

> The work is composed of three parts, entitled 'Apologetic', 'Dogmatic', and 'Moral'.
> The first comprises the rational principles of religion, the demonstration of Christian faith and the true Church of Jesus Christ, as well as the refutation of the principal errors.
> The second part unfolds the whole series of the dogmas of faith, from the mysteries of God and the creation to the universal judgment, the final term of God's work in this world.
> The third part presents an exposition of the Christian virtues and obligations. It treats of laws in general, of the Decalogue and the commandments of the Church, of sins and good works, of the Sacraments and of prayer, of the feasts and of religious ceremonies.[230]

The approach is typical of the period: based on first principles and definitions, somewhat legalistic in its moral teaching, relying to no great extent on Scripture. It is possible to find most of Stephen's questions touched on, but this is only to be expected. No claim is being entered that Fr Henry, much less the boys in his class, actually used the book, although this is perfectly possible. But if they used something else, the general approach was probably very similar. This particular copy of Schouppe was certainly used in 1881 to teach catechism classes (some sections are marked with a date), presumably in Belvedere; and school textbooks, catechisms perhaps especially, did not change very frequently at the time.

The extent to which Joyce's interests had focused by the end of his schooldays became apparent when the Senior Grade results were announced.[231] In all his subjects, with the sole exception of English, his marks had not merely dropped – they were the lowest he obtained in the four years that he had sat the examination. The Latin course included Livy V and the third book of Horace's *Odes* (as well as some of his *Epistles*). Stephen's 'timeworn Horace never felt cold to the touch even when his own fingers were cold' and 'the dusky verses were as fragrant as though they had lain all those years in myrtle and lavender and vervain' (442).[232] Joyce's admirable schoolboy rendering of Horace's thirteenth ode ('O fons Bandusiae') survives.[233] But he only got 560 for his examination papers. Mr McErlean's zeal on his behalf was not rewarded by a good mark in French. The texts were Erckmann-Chatrian's *L'Invasion* and Corneille's *Polyeucte*. Joyce got 345, like the Latin mark not quite 50 per cent. His Italian mark had fallen to 205.[234] In English he had had to read *Julius Caesar* and Macaulay's essays on Clive and Warren Hastings. The questions on 'the history of England and Ireland' extended to 1837; those on the 'history of English literature' to 1832. Among the latter was one which Joyce may have found to his taste: 'Point out some features common to the genius of Cowper, Crabbe, and Burns; *or* of Byron, Keats, and Shelley'. But it was no doubt in the composition that he once again scored most heavily. Two hundred and fifty marks and at least an hour of examination time were assigned to a composition on one of the following subjects:

(a)  The desirability of making hand and eye training an ordinary branch of school education.
(b)  'Men may rise on stepping-stones
     Of their dead selves, to higher things.'
(c)  The uses and abuses of Satire.
(d)  A Liberal Education.

With his liking for Newman, Joyce might have been tempted by the fourth topic. But it was, after all, Newman's prose rather than his theories that Stephen professed to admire. And, in any case, the second title may have harmonised very well with his sentiments as he prepared to leave school. Whichever essay he chose, he wrote well enough to win a £4 prize. Professor William Magennis, himself a past pupil of Belvedere and one of the examiners, thought that Joyce's paper was publishable.[235] With his lowest aggregate of marks since first entering for the Intermediate in 1894, he won no exhibition but he retained the award of the previous year.

The Jesuits in Belvedere, Fr Henry in particular, hardly perceived in these rather uneven results the portent they contained of the former sodality prefect's future career as one of the most gifted writers in the English language. There is no evidence that Joyce ever visited his old school again. His last sight of it was probably in August 1909. Briefly home from the continent, he went on a late-night walk through the city with Byrne. Their route back to 7 Eccles St, where Byrne was living, took them up North Great George's St to Belvedere, before turning down Denmark St towards Findlater's Church.[236] We have no

| Examination Number | STUDENT'S NAME AND ADDRESS | Greek | Latin | English | Commercial English | French |
|---|---|---|---|---|---|---|
| | MAXIMUM .. | 1200 | 1200 | 1200 | 400 | 700 |
| 6781 | Hamill, John, St. Mary's College (s. m.), Dundalk [**J.Ex.**'96] | 72 | 371 | 285 | × | 386 |
| 6782 | [Not Examined] | × | × | × | × | × |
| 6783 | [Failed] | × | × | 170 | × | 261 |
| 6784 | Harrington, Daniel, Christian Brothers' College, Cork [**J.Ex.**'96] | 550 | 557 | 840 | × | 390 |
| 6785 | Hayes, John J. I., Catholic Univ. Sch., 89 Lr. Leeson st., Dublin | 195 | 332 | 340 | × | 281 |
| 6786 | [Not Examined] | × | × | × | × | × |
| 6787 | Heaslett, George H., Royal School, Dungannon | 510 | 352 | 565 | × | 252 |
| 6788 | Herlihy, Daniel J., St. Brendan's Seminary, Killarney [**J.Ex.**'96] | 360 | 278 | 385 | × | 119 |
| 6789 | Hickman, Poole H., Grammar School, Tipperary [**J.Ex.**'96] | 235 | 181 | 270 | × | 311 |
| 6790 | Horgan, Michael J., Christian Schools, Cork [**J.Ex.**'96] | × | 225 | 305 | × | 228 |
| 6791 | Houghton, Kenneth A. H., Corrig School, Kingstown [**J.Ex.**'96] | × | 148 | 345 | × | 48 |
| 6792 | [Failed] | 30 | f | 70 | × | f |
| 6793 | Hurley, Timothy, St. Colman's College, Fermoy [**M.Ex.**'97] | 540 | 536 | 600 | × | 310 |
| 6794 | [Failed] | × | f | 310 | × | f |
| 6795 | Irwin, David, Campbell College, Belfast [**M.Ex.**'97] | × | 166 | 405 | × | 290 |
| 6796 | Irwin, William, St. Munchin's College, Limerick [**J.Ex.**'96] | 122 | 261 | 310 | × | 440 |
| 6797 | Jamison, Robert, Royal Academical Institution, Belfast | × | 527 | 445 | × | 142 |
| 6798 | Johnston, John, Royal School, Dungannon [**J.Ex.**'96] | 760 | 597 | 485 | × | 468 |
| 6799 | Jones, Christopher F., High School, Dublin [**J.Ex.**'96] | 285 | 374 | 240 | × | 302 |
| 6800 | Joyce, James A., Belvedere College (s.j.), Dublin [**M.Ex.**'97] | × | 560 | 650 | × | 345 |
| 6801 | [Failed] | f | f | 15 | × | 200 |
| 6802 | Kelly, Michael, Rockwell College (c. s. sp.), Cashel [**J.Ex.**'96] | × | 137 | 155 | f | 410 |
| 6803 | [Failed] | × | × | × | × | 231 |
| 6804 | Kelly, Patrick J., St. Mel's College, Longford | 15 | f | 85 | × | 42 |
| 6805 | Kelly (senior), Peter, St. Jarlath's College, Tuam [**J.Ex.**'96] | 390 | 467 | 225 | × | 115 |
| 6806 | Kelly (junior), Peter, St. Jarlath's College, Tuam [**J.Ex.**'96] | 550 | 337 | 330 | × | 236 |
| 6807 | Kennedy, Thomas, The College, Carlow [**J.Ex.**'96] | 490 | 518 | 245 | × | 320 |
| 6808 | Kennedy, William, St. Flannan's College, Ennis | 305 | 117 | 310 | × | 82 |
| 6809 | Kent, Edward T.. Christian Schs., N. Richmond st., Dublin[**M.Ex.**'97] | × | 232 | 240 | × | 466 |
| 6810 | Keohan, Edmund, Rockwell College (c. s. sp.), Cashel [**J.Ex.**'96] | × | 310 | 270 | × | 446 |
| 6811 | Kinahan, Robert J., St. Mary's Coll. (c. s. sp.), Rathmines[**M.Ex.**'97] | × | 514 | 425 | × | 410 |
| 6812 | [Not Examined] | × | × | × | × | × |
| 6813 | [Not Examined] | × | × | × | × | × |
| 6814 | [Not Examined] | × | × | × | × | × |
| 6815 | Lang. Martin A., St. Joseph's Seminary, Galway [**J.Ex.**'96] | × | 482 | 385 | 150 | 388 |
| 6816 | Lawless, James, St. Kieran's College, Kilkenny | 120 | 414 | 270 | × | 106 |
| 6817 | Leathem, George, Royal Academical Institution, Belfast [**M.Ex.**'97] | × | 532 | 940 | × | 305 |
| 6818 | Leen, John, Rockwell College (c. s. sp.), Cashel | 370 | 155 | 250 | × | 308 |
| 6819 | [Failed] | × | f | 45 | × | 59 |
| 6820 | Leitch, Andrew, Royal School, Dungannon | f | 62 | 75 | × | 91 |

Joyce's Intermediate results, 1898.

| Commercial French | German | Commercial German | Italian | Commercial Italian | Spanish | Commercial Spanish | Celtic | Algebra and Arithmetic | Euclid | Plane Trigonometry | Natural Philosophy | Chemistry | Drawing | Shorthand | Precis Writing | Total under Rule 57 | Examination Number |
|---|---|---|---|---|---|---|---|---|---|---|---|---|---|---|---|---|---|
| 200 | 700 | 200 | 500 | 200 | 500 | 200 | 600 | 900 | 600 | 700 | 500 | 500 | 500 | 300 | 200 | | |
| × | × | × | × | × | × | × | × | 100 | 60 | 15 | × | × | × | × | × | 1289 | 6781 |
| × | × | × | × | × | × | × | × | × | × | × | × | × | × | × | × | × | 6782 |
| × | × | × | × | × | × | × | × | f | 150 | f | × | × | × | × | × | 581 | 6783 |
| × | × | × | × | × | × | × | × | 260 | 150 | 195 | × | × | × | × | × | 2942 | 6784 |
| × | × | × | × | × | × | × | × | f | 155 | 30 | × | × | × | × | × | 1333 | 6785 |
| × | × | × | × | × | × | × | × | × | × | × | × | × | × | × | × | × | 6786 |
| × | × | × | × | × | × | × | × | P | 155 | f | × | × | × | × | × | 1834 | 6787 |
| × | × | × | × | × | × | × | × | 160 | 40 | f | × | , | × | × | × | 1342 | 6788 |
| × | × | × | × | × | × | × | × | 230 | 290 | 140 | × | 1 | × | × | × | 1657 | 6789 |
| × | × | × | × | × | × | × | 136 | P | 30 | f | × | × | × | f | 30 | 954 | 6790 |
| × | 92 | × | × | × | × | × | × | 120 | 245 | f | 160 | × | × | × | × | 1158 | 6791 |
| × | × | × | × | × | × | × | × | f | 25 | f | × | × | × | × | × | 125 | 6792 |
| × | × | × | × | × | × | × | × | 45 | 145 | 5 | × | × | × | × | × | 2181 | 6793 |
| × | × | × | × | × | × | × | × | f | 170 | 55 | 45 | × | f | × | × | 580 | 6794 |
| × | × | × | × | × | × | × | × | 380 | 490 | 135 | 180 | 208 | × | 50 | × | 2304 | 6795 |
| × | × | × | × | × | × | × | × | 110 | 235 | 105 | × | × | × | × | × | 1583 | 6796 |
| × | × | × | × | × | × | × | × | 330 | 190 | 275 | × | × | × | 30 | × | 1939 | 6797 |
| × | × | × | × | × | × | × | × | 370 | 190 | 250 | × | × | × | × | × | 3120 | 6798 |
| × | × | × | × | × | × | × | × | 610 | 220 | 440 | × | × | × | × | × | 2471 | 6799 |
| 102 | × | × | 205 | × | × | × | × | 145 | 40 | 20 | 10 | × | × | × | × | 2077 | 6800 |
| × | × | × | × | × | × | × | × | f | 130 | × | × | × | × | × | × | 345 | 6801 |
| 90 | × | × | × | × | × | × | × | 260 | 285 | P | × | × | × | × | × | 1337 | 6802 |
| × | × | × | × | × | × | × | × | 25 | × | 120 | × | × | × | × | × | 376 | 6803 |
| × | × | × | × | × | × | × | × | f | 65 | × | × | × | × | × | × | 207 | 6804 |
| × | × | × | × | × | × | × | × | 175 | 290 | 80 | × | × | × | × | × | 1743 | 6805 |
| × | × | × | × | × | × | × | × | f | 190 | 100 | × | × | × | × | × | 1743 | 6806 |
| × | × | × | × | × | × | × | × | 15 | 225 | f | × | × | × | × | × | 1813 | 6807 |
| × | × | × | × | × | × | × | × | f | 5 | × | × | × | × | × | × | 819 | 6808 |
| × | 335 | × | × | × | × | × | × | 310 | 160 | 5 | × | × | × | 18 | 60 | 1826 | 6809 |
| 77 | × | × | × | × | × | × | 240 | 265 | 350 | 430 | × | × | × | f | × | 2388 | 6810 |
| × | 342 | × | 256 | × | × | × | × | 345 | 155 | 110 | × | × | × | × | × | 2557 | 6811 |
| × | × | × | × | × | × | × | × | × | × | × | × | × | × | × | × | × | 6812 |
| × | × | × | × | × | × | × | × | × | × | × | × | × | × | × | × | × | 6813 |
| × | × | × | × | × | × | × | × | × | × | × | × | × | × | × | × | × | 6814 |
| × | × | × | × | × | × | × | × | 10 | 120 | 170 | × | × | × | × | × | 1705 | 6815 |
| × | × | × | × | × | × | × | × | 40 | 90 | f | × | × | × | × | × | 1040 | 6816 |
| × | 201 | × | × | × | × | × | × | 900 | 600 | 490 | 225 | × | × | × | × | 4193 | 6817 |
| × | × | × | × | × | × | × | × | 95 | 75 | f | × | × | × | × | × | 1253 | 6818 |
| × | × | × | × | × | × | × | × | f | 50 | f | × | × | × | × | × | 154 | 6819 |
| × | × | × | × | × | × | × | × | 50 | 35 | f | × | × | × | × | × | 313 | 6820 |

141

record of his thoughts on that occasion, but he had already shadowed forth in his mind and in *Stephen Hero* the double-edged portrait of his school which he later consolidated in *A Portrait of the Artist as a Young Man*. No past pupil of Belvedere would ever describe so painstakingly what it was like to be at school there and, however far he removed himself from it both geographically and spiritually in later life, James Joyce never disavowed the powerful influence that his years at Belvedere had had upon him.

# References

Introduction (pp. 1–8)

1. Quoted in Ellmann, p. 153.
2. *The Clongownian*, December 1899, p. 26.
3. Gorman, p. 62.
4. *The Clongownian*, 1920, pp. 38–42.
5. Ibid., 1921, pp. 201–08.
6. Ibid., 1930, pp. 31–33. In his contribution to *A Page of Irish History*, published the same year, Clery, then a professor of law at UCD, felt able to be more explicit. Remarking on how the Gaelic revival, 'by giving us students an ideal, raised the tone of our lives, and an exceptionally high moral standard prevailed among us', he added in a footnote: 'Readers of Mr James Joyce will get a different impression, but this is the actual fact. . . . Joyce is true as far as he goes, but confining himself to one small knot of medical students he gives a wrong impression of the whole' (pp. 585–86). On Clery's contacts with Joyce at university, see Ellmann pp. 72–75, 93–94; Sullivan, *passim*. Clery was one of the few Irish reviewers of Joyce's first major published work, *Chamber Music* (Ellmann, p. 271).
7. John Horgan, 'Clongowes 1893–97', *The Clongownian*, 1955, pp. 9–13. The editor was the present rector of Belvedere, Fr Paul Andrews, then a scholastic in Clongowes. The magazine contained a passing reference to Joyce in 1964 (pp. 9–10). In 1970, one of the boys, Master P. McDonnell, compiled a list of 'interesting points about Clongowes'. The fourteenth 'interesting point' was that 'James Joyce who wrote *Ulysses* is a past pupil' (p. 47).
8. *The Belvederian*, 1907, p. 71. Verse contributions were not usually quite so anonymous but contained at least the writer's initials.
9. See below, p. 106.
10. *The Belvederian*, 1910, p. 182.
11. Ibid., 1924, p. 24. On Dawson and Joyce in UCD, see Sullivan, p. 203.
12. Ibid., 1957, pp. 71–73.
13. Ibid., 1959, pp. 108–09.
14. Ibid., 1960, pp. 58–59. The photograph was supplied and the identifications made by Col. Jack Burke-Gaffney, whose older brother was in the photograph.
15. Ibid., 1907, p. 58; also the list of Mr Dempsey's prizewinners below (p. 132).
16. Ibid., 1957, p. 73.
17. Quoted in Noon, p. 1.

18. Hutchins, p. 22.
19. Ibid.
20. Ellmann, p. 30.
21. Scholes & Kain, p. 138.
22. On *The Rhetorician*, see *The Clongownian*, June 1900, pp. 19–21; December 1900, pp. 24–25.
23. Ellmann, facing p. 49.
24. Tindall, pp. 28–29; 30–31.
25. Anderson, pp. 14–15.
26. Ellmann, p. 283.
27. The most valuable source of photographs of Clongowes in Joyce's time is an album containing classes and other groups taken in 1888–92, together with views of the college at this period. The picture of Joyce with his Elements class of 1888–89 has been published once before, in the *Irish Rosary*, 16 (1962), p. 215.
28. Anderson, ed., p. 491 has noticed how the first episode covers twenty-four hours. The second episode also extends over a day, if the accident on the cinderpath and other events in the school the day before are included in the twenty-four-hour period.
29. The first chapter is 'not a record of actual events recollected in maturity; it is the imaginative recording of a series of immediate impressions' (Sullivan, p. 41).
30. According to Joyce's 'Notes for *Stephen Hero*' (published in Scholes & Kain, pp. 68–73), the Whitsuntide play takes place in May or June 1893, with Stephen's rivalry with Vincent Heron, the issue of his own essays and the subsequent 'fight with Heron' all set in the months between February and June of that year. The journey to Cork and a significant sexual experience are located in the summer holidays (between June and September 1893). What the notes call 'gradual irreligiousness' belongs to this period too, followed by the return to the 'second class' in September, when Stephen becomes prefect of the sodality, and the retreat before the feast of St Francis Xavier in December. If Stephen Dedalus was born in 1882, like James Joyce, he was not twelve at the end of 1893. These are certainly not historically accurate dates for the corresponding events in Joyce's life. The visit to Cork took place early in 1894. The rivalry with Albrecht Connolly ('Heron') etc. and Joyce's first sexual experiences probably belong to 1895–96. Joyce entered 'number two' (Middle Grade) and became sodality prefect in September 1896 and the retreat took place in December of the same year. His gradual 'irreligiousness' seems to date from some time in 1897. The Whitsuntide play took place in 1890. On this period in Joyce's life, see chapter two below.
31. *A Portrait*, p. 417: 'The echoes of certain expressions used in Clongowes sounded in remote caves of his mind.'
32. Gorman, p. 27.
33. Sullivan, p. 2.
34. Gorman, p. 27     35. Ibid., p. 37.
36. Chapter two, pp. 310, 311, 319, 334, 336, 343; chapter three, p. 361;

chapter four, pp. 415–16, 421; chapter five, p. 436.

37. In the Martello Tower in the morning (p. 12); on Sandymount Strand later (pp. 49, 57); in the *Freeman* office at noon (p. 171); at the National Library after lunch (p. 242); in the maternity hospital in the late evening (p. 543); in the brothel at midnight (p. 667); in Bloom's house in the small hours (p. 781).

38. Belvedere is mentioned by name only six times in *A Portrait*; Joyce sometimes uses 'the college' instead. The only allusion in the final chapter is Stephen's recollection of Fr Henry's Latin class, as he passes Trinity on his way to UCD. Belvedere is not mentioned at all in *Ulysses*. During the afternoon, in Bedford Row, Stephen looks through the volumes on a bookcart and muses: 'I might find here one of my pawned schoolprizes. *Stephano Dedalo, alumno optimo, palmam ferenti*' (311). But this formula was used for prizegiving in both schools. In *Finnegans Wake*, Joyce mentions 'The Belvedarean exhibitioners. In their cruisery caps and oarsclub colours' (205). He also recalls: 'We've had our day at triv and quad and writ our bit as intermidgets' (306). He alludes to Clongowes more obscurely, speaking of 'a tibertine's pile with a Congoswood cross on the back for Sunny Twimjim' (211). He liked to play on the formulas he had learned at the beginning and end of his exercises in Clongowes and Belvedere (see *A Portrait*, p. 317; Ellmann pp. 36–37): 'At maturing daily gloryaims! Lawdy Dawdy Simpers' (282); 'Ellers for the greeter glossary of code' (324).

39. Quoted in Ellmann, p. 27.

40. Sullivan, p. 148.

Chapter 1: Clongowes Wood College 1888–91 (pp. 9–83)

1. This was the official 'return day' in 1888, according to the *Prefect's Journal*, although only about half of the boys came back on that day. It may be presumed that a new boy like Joyce was among them.

2. 'Father Conmee and his associates' in Ryan, ed., p. 150. O'Mahony states that the minister of Clongowes in 1888, Fr Thomas P. Brown (who had just ceased to be provincial of the Irish Jesuits) was 'a friend of the Joyce family' (ibid.). Fr Brown's letter to Mrs Joyce about 'Jim' on 9 March 1889 (in Ellmann, p. 28) could be construed on that basis. But O'Mahony offers no evidence for his statement.

3. O'Mahony, *loc. cit.*; Ellmann, p. 16. Conmee was actually born at Glanduff near Athlone and not Kingsland as O'Mahony asserts (according to his own statement in *Informations of the Novices*).

4. Carlow College (1791) was older but more a seminary than a lay school.

5. M. Sweetman, S.J., 'Clongowes Aims 1814–1964', *The Clongownian*, 1964, p. 7. Samuel Lewis, *A Topographical Dictionary of Ireland*, London 1837, described it as 'a college for the education of the sons of the Catholic nobility and gentry' (p. 328). The circumstances of Clongowes' foundation are confusing and it is not too surprising that Fr Conmee gave the foundation date as 1813 in his 1886 Prospectus. The matter is

clarified in R. Burke Savage, S.J., 'Founders' Day 4 March 1814', *The Clongownian*, 1981, pp. 3–12.

6. Manuscript in Province Archives.

7. T. Morrissey, S.J., unpublished thesis, p. 390. The three Catholic laymen appointed to the Intermediate Board (Chief Baron Palles, The O'Conor Don and Lord O'Hagan) were all old Clongownians (ibid., p. 414). See Morrisey's forthcoming publication *In the Gallery of Nation-Builders: Dr William Delany, S. J. ( 1883–87; 1897–1908)*.

8. *The Clongownian*, 1914, p. 32.

9. See Morrissey, p. 431.

10. Mr Dedalus wanted his son 'to mix with gentlemen' (341) and felt that the Jesuits, rather than the Christian Brothers, were the ones to ensure that. The word 'gentleman' recurs throughout most of *A Portrait* as an ironic counterpoint to the declining family fortunes.

11. According to the *Students' Register*, Saurin was born on 20 July 1876, Christopher ('Nasty') Roche on 31 August 1877, Cecil Thunder on 24 June 1878, Rody Kickham on 20 November 1878, Tom Furlong on 26 October 1879, and Jack Lawton on 14 December 1880. Joyce was born on 2 February 1882.

12. Stanislaus Joyce, quoted in Sullivan, p. 14. The prospectus, which Sullivan prints, stated, 'Boys are received from the age of seven' (ibid., p. 233).

13. Ellmann, p. 26.

14. Sullivan, p. 231. The Prospectus also promised: 'Special care is taken of very young boys. They have the benefit of female attendance, and the dietary and studies are modified to suit their tender years' (ibid., p. 233).

15. *My Brother's Keeper*, p. 60.

15a. *The Parliamentary Gazeteer of Ireland* says of Clongowes, 'The *tout ensemble* of its architectural features suggests the idea of a tasteless and almost random combination of castle, gaol, and church' (p. 445). The description might have appealed to Stephen Dedalus, if not to Joyce.

16. As the *Leinster Leader* noted with approval on 6 June 1887. Over the years *The Clongownian* has published occasional articles of reminiscence, containing descriptions of the school as it was in an earlier era.

17. G. R. Roche was born on 21 November 1869 and was a seventeen-year-old member of First Arts when Joyce came to Clongowes. He should not be confused with Christopher ('Nasty') Roche who was only eleven and in the Third Line. Anderson, ed., pp. 485 and 491 makes this mistake, followed by Benstock and Benstock, p. 147.

18. Sullivan, p. 31. He gives Fr P. A. Baggot, rector of Clongowes 1953–59, as his source for George Roche's evidence.

19. Sullivan, pp. 42–43.

20. *Students' Ledger*, f. 132.

21. Sullivan, pp. 31, 43.

22. *Students' Register*.

23. Slippers, gloves and a prayerbook in the half year from February 1889, costing 8/4 all told.

24. See below, pp. 37, 74.
25. See note 22 above. There were forty-one in this dormitory and thirty-five (including Saurin) in the Third Line dormitory (for older boys) below. Over in the Lower Line dormitory there were as many as 106 (including S. Little, A. Kickham, D. Kelly and J. Magee) and sixty-three (including P. Rath) in the Higher Line dormitory. These rooms were on the second floor of the buildings constructed in 1821, at right-angles to the Castle, between the study hall and the 1819 Boys' Chapel. The figures given here make a total of 255. Joyce's figure in *Stephen Hero* (p. 165) of 300 is too high. Numbers seem to have oscillated between about 230 and 260 in his time.
26. The information in this paragraph is drawn from the *Prefect's Journal* kept in that year by Fr Henry Lynch (not to be confused with his name-sake, quoted in note 6 above). The month of September is fairly fully recorded, but after that the journal peters out.
27. *'A mistake'*, the journal observes.
28. There are three versions of these 'Rules of the Boys of Clongoweswood' in the Clongowes Archives, one considerably older than the version Joyce heard and one revised again in 1931. The rules in force at the end of the century are harsher and more authoritarian in tone than the earlier version. Thomas Emerson, who came to Clongowes from Galway in 1886, wrote: 'The first thing that impressed me was the multiplicity of the rules' (*The Rhetorician*, 13 February 1891).
29. The same 'Rules' were read at the beginning of each new year. Joyce would have heard them read by Fr Henry Fegan in September 1889 and 1890. Fr Henry Lynch was minister in 1891.
30. A number of the boys, as the dates given in the text show, arrived late in the academic year 1888–89. Richard Martin did not come till 30 May, too late for the photograph. Eugene Kenny left on 1 April and he is not in the photograph either. The other absentee is John Cantwell, who was in the school but may have been sick when the photograph was taken, presumably some time in April or May.
31. Dates are from Corcoran. The addresses are from the *Students' Register* and the *Students' Ledger*.
32. Joyce's address occurs five times in the *Register*. It has been erroneously included in an index of names and addresses for 1887–88 where it is given as 43 Fleet Street (Collector-General's office). The index for 1888–89 has the same address. The Elements class-list for 1889–90 has 1 Martello Terrace, Bray. Both addresses are given in an index for 1890–91. The Rudiments class-list for 1891–92 gives Leoville House, Blackrock, Co. Dublin. The *Ledger* has the Fleet Street address from 1888 and the Martello Terrace address has been added in 1890.
33. See *A Portrait*, p. 333: 'The voice of his school comrades urged him to be a decent fellow, to shield others from blame. . . .'
34. But writes 'Roderick', by mistake for Rodolph (318). Kickham had greaves 'in his number' (247). This is possibly a reference to the 'magazine' or trunk-room, off the old Long Gallery on the left-hand side, just short of the entrance to the square. The boys only retained articles

for immediate use in the dormitory; otherwise they went to the magazine and were issued with what they required from their 'number'. Rody Kickham shared number 164 with his brother. Joyce's number was 63. Numbers seem to have been assigned randomly (*Students' Register*).

35. 1934, p. 94.
36. He and Cecil Thunder entered the novitiate, then at Tullabeg, on 7 September 1895. Thunder left on 14 September 1896 and Kickham on 29 April 1897. His brother Alexander, obscurely referred to in *A Portrait*, had already entered the novitiate on 6 September 1890 along with Dominic Kelly. He refers in *Informations of the Novices* to three brothers and three sisters living and three brothers already dead. His father was also dead. He speaks of himself as 'not very strong' and he died 'of influenza' on 30 April 1892. (Information drawn from documents in the Province Archives.)
37. 1934, p. 94.    38. See note 17 above.
39. *Students' Register*. Hodgart has rightly noted that 'the last section of the first chapter ... is told in the style of a schoolboy's story' (p. 61). Compare *A Portrait*, p. 298 and Arnold Lunn's *The Harrovians*, p. 14: 'Thomson says he raised his hand above his shoulder, which is against the law.' But there are echoes of the same style (hence the same suggestion of parody) in the second section of the chapter. Compare 'Nasty' Roche's questioning and Stephen's reply with Lunn, p. 7: 'As he strolled up the Trollope House drive he knew exactly what to expect. He would, of course, be surrounded by half-hostile critics. "What's your father?" some ill-favoured lout would ask, to which he would retort with a variation of the traditional reply, "My father was a gentleman; what was yours?"' Anderson, ed., p. 507 finds echoes of Anstey's school story, *Vice Versa*, in Vincent Heron's language in the third chapter of *A Portrait*.
40. See below, p. 37.
41. The 'square ditch' is not to be confused with the 'square', an error repeated in Anderson, ed., p. 488. The 'square ditch', better known as 'Nelly's ditch', was described by Thomas Francis Meagher in 1842 as follows: 'There was Nelly's ditch, with its scant supply of lazy water, full of frogs' blankets, weeds, pinkeens, and dock leaves – the same old dismal ditch it was some thirty years ago. Thirty years ago it received the name it bears. An old woman of the name of Nelly, being very blind and helpless, walked into it one winter's morning, on her way back from the chapel to the laundry, and remained there until it was useless to take her out. It served as a fosse for one face of the castle ...' (*The Clongownian*, 1914, p. 26). It would have been physically impossible for Wells to have shouldered Stephen 'into' the latrine, which is what 'the square' means. It would also have been highly illegal for them to have carried on a conversation of any kind there (see p. 68 below).
42. Anderson, ed., p. 490, makes the cross-reference to Stephen's discussion with Cranly about a mother's love and St Aloysius Gonzaga's refusal to be kissed by his mother in the fifth chapter of *A Portrait*.

43. See *A Portrait,* p. 303 where Stephen tells his story to Fr Conmee: 'A fellow was coming out of the bicycle house and I fell and they got broken. I don't know the fellow's name.' In Belvedere, he hears 'the voice of his school comrades to be a decent fellow, to shield others from blame or to beg them off. . . .' (333).

44. He had been absent for long periods, including most of the spring of 1890 (from 22 February to 17 April), probably due to ill health, as charges for medical attention in his account would suggest (*Students' Ledger*). Wells appears as a clerical student in Clonliffe in *Stephen Hero,* whom Stephen, then at University College, Dublin, meets in North Richmond St (pp. 66–71). He strikes an attitude of false heartiness. Stephen sees him later chanting Tenebrae in the Pro-Cathedral (p. 108). Stephen 'felt impulses of pity' for him, along with his mother and others (p. 116). It has not been possible to verify whether Charles Wells ever was a student in Clonliffe, though it must be very probable. He does not appear to have been ordained.

45. James Davy's father was a Justice of the Peace in Swords and William Hannin's in Banagher (*Students' Ledger*).

46. In Clongowes with his brother John (1889–91) and listed in Corcoran, p. 198. The MacSwineys lived in Essex.

47. Address, 28 Rathmines Road, Dublin.

48. Ellmann, p. 30, who adds: 'Word went round that "Furlong and Joyce will not for long rejoice"', a pun Joyce liked in later life.

49. See the photograph of the cast (p. 56).

50. See below, p. 47ff.

51. Listed for Rudiments in 1889–90 and Preparatory Grade in 1891–92 (*Students' Register*). No list for 1890–91, but he would probably have been in Third of Grammar. Address, 9 Brookfield Terrace, Donnybrook, Dublin.

52. Ale or porter at £2 and wine at £3 were available to the older boys in the refectory. It has to be remembered that 'older boys' could be of university graduation age at the time, as Clongowes offered teaching up to that level.

53. See note 39 above.

54. *A Page of Irish History,* p. 610.

55. See note 36 above.

56. Corcoran, *Clongowes Record.*

57. The register of classes was not kept for that year. Fr Daly was unwell in the winter, as the general's correspondence with the provincial shows.

57a. For this and all other identifications of Joyce's pseudonyms, see Sullivan, *passim.*

58. *The Clongownian,* 1913, pp. 422–23.

59. He died on 21 January 1914, aged thirty-four. An obituary appeared in *The Clongownian,* 1914, p. 159. Of boys mentioned by Joyce, his was one of the few careers charted over the years in the school magazine. Cecil Thunder's death on 30 November 1909 (aged thirty-one) was reported in 1910 (p. 337) but there was no obituary. Similarly with Michael Saurin (1922, p. 315) and Tom Furlong (1933, p. 91).

60. Anderson, ed., p. 489, says 'The soutanes of the Jesuits in Joyce's day had a piece of material hanging from each shoulder down the back.' The Irish and English Jesuits, in the earliest photographs, wear a distinctive sleeveless gown which has the false sleeves referred to above. This gown is peculiar to these two provinces and is still worn today. Boys still do what Simon Moonan did with the false sleeves. 'Suck' means sycophant, as Anderson suggests (ibid.) – the modern equivalent is 'lick', to convey which the boys make a sucking sound.

61. Thus Anderson, ed., p. 486; Richard M. Kain, 'Epiphanies of Dublin' in Staley and Benstock, p. 111, n. 9. Sullivan, p. 48, does not realise that Fleming is a pseudonym.

62. *Students' Register.*

63. Ellmann, p. 31, footnote.

64. Anderson, ed., p. 486, mistakenly includes Barnes and Flowers, who were not boys but cricket coaches from England. Not surprisingly, he cannot find their names in the *Clongowes Record* (p. 497). This mistake has been followed by Benstock and Benstock who describe Barnes as 'reputed candidate for Clongowes cricket team captaincy' (p. 51), and Flowers as 'master at Clongowes Wood' (p. 89). See below, p. 51.

65. Sullivan, p. 48.

66. Fr Paddy Crowe S.J. suggests that Athy is in fact Jeremiah O'Neill, who was in Clongowes, 1888–91, and was the only boy from Athy there in that period. O'Neill was actually already in Second of Grammar in 1888–89 and either in the Lower Line or in the Higher Line (*Students' Register*). According to his obituary in *The Clongownian*, 1955, p. 25, he was already fifteen when he came to Clongowes. It is possible that Athy was a nickname actually used by the other boys at the time, so that it is not a pseudonym in the strict sense.

67. *The Clongownian*, 1912, p. 239.

68. Ibid., pp. 239–40.

69. Ibid., p. 239.

70. Reported in George Roche's obituary, *The Clongownian*, 1937, p. 13. This obituary, from which some of the information in the text is drawn, was one of four devoted to Rath, covering six pages (13–18). He had been one of the school's most esteemed past pupils, very active in the St Vincent de Paul Society (to relieve poverty) and the Past Pupils' Union of which he had been president, once he returned to Dublin. He spent his first years after leaving school 'managing a large farm with 22,000 sheep, 1,500 cattle, and some 200 horses' in Buenos Aires (*The Clongownian*, Christmas 1897, p. 46). He wrote an account of this for the school magazine in 1900 (pp. 14–17). There is a garbled reference to 'Roth [*sic*] . . . out in Australia now – bushranger or something' in *Stephen Hero*, p. 67. Paddy Rath has several Dublin addresses successively in the *Students' Register*. The first appears to be 39 Merville Place, Kingstown.

71. Ellmann, p. 28.

72. *The Clongownian*, 1912, p. 239. The Magees lived at 8 Rathmines Terrace, Dublin.

73. Rath, Magee and others of their generation in Tullabeg and Clongowes subsequently had long and distinguished careers in senior clubs, many of them going on to represent their country as 'Gentlemen of Ireland'. Joseph Molony was their predecessor as captain (1888–90), followed by Thomas Ross in January 1890.

74. *Students' Register, Students' Ledger.* According to the 'Rules', 'the use of tobacco is strictly forbidden except in certain special cases when a privilege be granted to some of the more grown boys'. The *Punishment Book* records normally heavy punishment for breaches of this rule.

75. See p. 31.

76. *The Clongownian*, 1913, pp. 425–26. Anderson, ed., p. 486 failed to find a Portuguese name in Corcoran.

77. Both were exhibitioners from Junior to Senior Grade. On entering the Society of Jesus, Kickham wrote that 'for the past six years the glands about the neck and cheeks have been swollen considerably' (*Informations of the Novices*). This condition is obvious in contemporary photographs.

78. *Students' Register.*

79. See note 36 above.

80. Sullivan prints the concert programme (p. 234). Ignatius Little left sick from Second of Grammar in May 1890, shortly after the concert and seven months before his brother's death.

81. Kelly, who came from 1 Priest's Road, Tramore, Co. Waterford, persevered as a Jesuit, returning to Clongowes as a scholastic from 1902–04 and later as a priest from 1910–17. He was a very gifted man who taught practically all the subjects in the curriculum in Clongowes and later in Australia, where he was transferred in 1917. He was also a keen photographer, even while at school. He died in 1952 (see *Province News*, October 1952, pp. 104–05). Apart from Alex Kickham, four other Clongownians – Henry Gill, James Kirwan, Laurence Potter and Tim Corcoran – became Jesuits in 1890 and all persevered. Gill was an older brother of the two boys who were in Elements with Joyce in 1888.

82. *de more*: 'as usual'. This journal is the source for information about orders of time. It was more concerned to note variations, which were quite frequent, than the norm, but the timetable given in the text seems to have been the basic pattern.

83. Information in this and the succeeding paragraphs is based on articles in *The Clongownian*, 1924, pp. 24–27; 1932, pp. 13–19; 1944, pp. 74–76; 1960, pp. 6–12.

84. E. J. Gannon (1877–82), *The Clongownian*, 1914, p. 34; Herbert Devine (1896–1900), ibid., p. 61; P. McGlade (1904–09), ibid., 1960, p. 10.

85. *The Rhetorician*, 17 May 1888. Forrest was in Clongowes, 1886–88.

86. Fr T. P. Brown, 1888–89; Fr Henry Fegan, 1889–91; Fr Henry Lynch, 1891–92.

87. *The Clongownian*, 1960, p. 10. According to J. J. Horgan (1893–97), 'raids on their overladen tables in the refectory were not unknown', *The Clongownian*, 1955, p. 11. But there were special days when all the boys ate in style. The feast to celebrate the Intermediate results has been mentioned (p. 16). At Hallowe'en 1889, the *Minister's Journal* says: 'Nuts, apples and tipsy cake for all the boys'.

88. The 'Rules' laid down that 'All are to wash, comb and brush their hair twice a day – in the morning when they rise and at midday washing. All should be careful to have their nails and teeth always clean.' In view of Joyce's practice at a later stage, this early training in hygiene is not without irony.

89. Born in Dundalk in 1863. He spent only two years in Clongowes, 1888–90.

90. *A Portrait*, pp. 246, 250, 253.

91. Elsewhere applied by Stephen to Rody Kickham (246), Fleming (252) and Mr Harford (290); by Athy to Bro. Michael (265) and by Third Line companions to Fr Conmee, 'the decentest rector that was ever in Clongowes' (305).

92. Sullivan, p. 43, thinks that 'he had probably received his first instructions from Mr Macardle'.

93. *Punishment Book* is the source of these and all other references to boys being punished, unless otherwise stated.

94. *Students' Ledger*, f. 132.

95. Hence it is a measure of Fleming's anger on Stephen's behalf that he says of the unjust pandying by 'Baldyhead' Dolan: 'It's a stinking mean low trick, that's what it is' (298).

96. *The Clongownian*, 1960, p. 9. Anderson, ed., p. 489, erroneously asserts that Fr William Power was 'master of the elements grade during Joyce's time in Clongowes'. He held the position only for one year. Similarly, Sullivan p. 36, presumes that Power, Macardle and Jeffcoat retained their 1888 functions 'during Joyce's time', which is a mistake.

97. *Informations of the Novices*.

98. Sullivan, pp. 36–37.

99. His health was always poor and he died in 1908. His obituary spoke of him as 'a very gentle, lovable, refined man' (*Menology of the Irish Province of the Society of Jesus*).

100. The *Punishment Book* was for recording these notes. In fact, Mr Barrett's name occurs only once in the *Punishment Book*, but it was not well kept for much of the time he was in Clongowes. Anderson, ed., p. 494, follows Sullivan's error (p. 72) in stating that Mr Barrett was not in Clongowes.

101. See Schwickerath, pp. 511–21.

102. Letters of Fr General to Fr Provincial, 18 October 1895 and 19 November 1895.

103. *The Clongownian*, 1932, p. 87.

104. Morrissey, p. 311. See Schwickerath, p. 515.

105. The photograph is on p. 42.

106. Conversation in Clongowes, 23 July 1976. *The Rhetorician*, 17 May 1888 reported an expedition to Lucan by the Choir, 'under the management of Father Power and Mr Eyre': 'The course of their expedition ... did not run smooth, as the first-named gentleman kept continually getting into embroglios with them.' From Tullabeg, William Power published a volume of erudite yet childishly sentimental verses entitled *The King's Bell and Other Verses* (Braine-le-Comte, Belgium, 1910).

107. See chapter two below.

108. See Sullivan, pp. 130–31.

109. Ibid., pp. 42–45.

110. This can be seen from entries in the *Punishment Book*.

111. *Punishment Book*.

112. From 'most recent directions concerning (1857–1858) the matter to be taught in each class – by Revd. Joseph Lentaigue Rect(or) and Pref(ect) of Stud(ies)' in *The Prefect of Studies C. W. C. Custom Book*. This was not maintained by his successors and Fr Daly, in particular, seems to have kept no records apart from the *Students' Register*.

113. Sullivan, p. 47. His error has been followed by Ellmann (p. 29).

114. Ibid., p. 14. On the length of Joyce's stay in Clongowes, see below, pp. 78–80.

115. Corpus Christi might have been the expected day, but it is clear from the *Prefect's Journal* and the *Minister's Journal* that the procession happened on the feast of the Sacred Heart. The 'little wood' is the so-called 'pleasure ground' to the left of the Castle, viewed from the front avenue. Fr Fegan gives the following information in the *Minister's Journal* for Friday 13 June: 'Feast of Sd Heart ... 7 (p.m.) (sharp) Procession. *Route* as last year. Playground door, Ha ha, skirt pleasure ground by farmyard road – in through iron gate and up centre walk'.

116. *A Portrait*, p. 284: 'How could they have done that? He thought of the dark silent sacristy. .... It was in the chapel but still you had to speak under your breath. It was a holy place.'

117. Joyce's account in the *Students' Ledger*, f. 132 contains the following entry for 2 September 1889: 'P(rayer)-book 2/6, gloves 8d'. Compare the entry for Charles Wells, who is also charged for a first communion medal (costing 10/9) along with the other two items, f. 324. In Joyce's case the medal may have been supplied from home or lent by the school. There was a special *Clongowes Registry of Confirmations and First Communions* but it was not maintained between 1881 and 1892. On 12 June 1892, John Lawton of Midleton received his first communion and was also confirmed the same day. Lawton, however, was eleven and a half in 1892. Gorman p. 37, says that 'before he left', Joyce 'was received definitively into the bosom of the church by the rite of Confirmation and took Aloysius for his saint's name'. (St Aloysius was the patron of Clongowes.) This presumably took place in June 1891.

118. *The Clongownian*, 1960, p. 9. The Boys' Chapel also served as a chapel-of-ease for the parish of Clane. According to Samuel Lewis, in his entry headed 'Mainham', it had been the actual parish church. But Anderson, ed., p. 491, is wrong in thinking that it was still so in Joyce's time.

119. Sullivan, p. 33. He is mistaken about Bro. Hanly being sacristan or having anything to do with Joyce as a server. Hanly, according to the *Catalogus,* was sacristan of the 'domestic chapel', the Jesuits' private chapel in the Castle, not of the Boys' Chapel.

120. If he served with George Roche, as Sullivan, p. 33, seems to imply, this would have been before Roche left in the summer of 1889.

120a. 'Gamekeepers and Shopkeepers' were the boys in charge of games in their line and helpers in the shop, at the junction of the two main galleries.

121. There would have been few, if any, 'Tullabeggars' in the Third Line and certainly none in Joyce's class. But the impact of the 1886 amalgamation, which amounted in many ways to a suppression of Tullabeg, could still be felt in Joyce's time and afterwards. *The Rhetorician*, 28 April 1888, commenting on a suggested expedition to the old school, wrote: 'A great many fellows would like to see old Tullabeg again, while others who have never been there are anxious to see what it is like. We, for one, should be very averse to such an idea. It would be awakening old recollections and reminiscences which would only tend to sadden – which would not be nice on a day of enjoyment.' Many of the prominent Higher Line boys, including Paddy Rath, had been in Tullabeg. The younger boys in Clongowes were naturally curious about the place and this is the significance of the prefect 'telling them something about Tullabeg' (*A Portrait*, p. 253).

122. See note 50 above.

123. Information in this paragraph is from articles in *The Clongownian*, 1903, p. 21; 1913, pp. 345–56; and 1944, p. 76.

124. *My Brother's Keeper*, p. 61.

125. G. R. Roche in *The Clongownian*, 1908, p. 123.

126. The *Prefect's Journal* shows this for the 1891–92 season.

127. *Prefect's Journal*, April 1890; *The Clongownian*, 1960, pp. 10–11.

128. *My Brother's Keeper*, p. 61.

129. *The Clongownian*, 1955, p. 12.

130. *Prefect's Journal*, 17 March 1890; G. R. Roche, *The Clongownian*, 1908, p. 123.

131. According to Paddy Rath, *The Clongownian*, 1912, p. 238, Shacklock of Notts came in the summer of 1887, followed by Barnes in 1888 and 1889, and Flowers in 1890 and 1891. *The Rhetorician*, 28 April 1888, chronicled the arrival of Barnes in its 'Gossip' column on the front page, under the heading 'The Prof'. It commented that 'he has of course . . . been used in sporting columns as the medium of advertisement for much trumpeted Clongowes'. A later item in the same issue regretted the poor weather, inimical to the playing of cricket, 'considering so much money had been spent on the Prof'.

132. See *The Clongownian*, June 1903, p. 21. The 'Rules' contain an appendix (which would not have been read out in the refectory) of regulations for the 'Clongowes Bicycle Club'. Stephen later remembers 'some jesuits . . . walking round the cycletrack in the company of ladies' (*A Portrait*, p. 417).

133. See *Prefect's Journal*.

134. See above, pp. 28–29.

135. *My Brother's Keeper*, p. 61.

136. *The Clongownian*, p. 11. 'Places of historic interest' would have included Hamilton Rowan's house at nearly Rathcoffey and Wolfe Tone's grave at Bodenstown. Stephen Dedalus knows about both.

137. Major Barton's estate was near Straffan and a familiar venue on walks.

137a. 'Those who cannot swim must keep to the shallow end' ('Rules': Swimming Bath).

138. *The Clongownian*, June 1896, p. 23. There may be a reminiscence of Fr Power's drill in the prefect's cry, 'Quick march! Hayfoot! Strawfoot!' to Stephen, as he leads him to the infirmary (*A Portrait*, p. 263).

139. The items are entered as: 'Music 1/6/3 Piano 2/6 Pieces 4/–' (1 February 1891) and 'Music 2/12/6 P(ieces) 5/–' (1 September 1891). 'Music' meant the instruction and 'Piano' meant 'use of the piano'. The February charges are, in each instance, at half price. The section of the 'Rules' concerning 'private lessons' evidently referred to music, and were simply common sense.

140. *The Clongownian*, 1935, p. 44.

141. Information about the play is taken from William Butler's review, referred to below in the text. Sullivan incorrectly refers to the play as 'Aladdin and the Wonderful Scamp' (pp. 50, 235). According to Butler, the play 'was not altogether a stranger to Clongowes audiences. It is said that in Fr Conmee's youth it was produced in the old theatre and that he filled one of the chief parts with great success'.

142. A separate photograph exists of the ten 'mandarins' mentioned in the programme.

143. *The Rhetorician*, April 1891.

144. Ibid., Ellmann (p. 30) refers to Joyce having sung at a Third Line concert 'about 1890'.

145. Ellmann, p. 27.

146. The account sent out in September 1891, and retrospective for items of this kind, includes 'Med(ical) Att(ention) 8/6'. There were apparently measles in Clongowes around this time (*The Rhetorician*, April 1891); perhaps this is why Joyce had the doctor.

147. For which some got eight and some twelve.

148. 20 November 1888. He got six on this occasion, but twelve in February.

149. 'No one may enter the Infirmary on any pretence whatever, even in case of illness, without first obtaining leave from the Minister, or if he cannot be found, from the Higher Line Prefect.'

150. A lampoon of Fr Daly in *The Rhetorician*, 17 May 1888, has him saying 'excitedly': 'Are you sure he is not foxing, Doctor? Oh give me some hope, oh say he is, and I'll soon have him up and doing. Don't you, don't you think he's foxing?'

151. When Bro. Hanly died on 25 January 1897, *The Clongownian* obituary asked: 'What Past man is there, for years back, who will not miss the kindly word and smile of old Brother Hanly? Instinctively their thoughts will go back to the time when as boys they sought his aid for their real or imaginary – more often the latter – pains and aches, and few indeed were the ailments his skilful treatment could not drive away' (June 1897, p. 7). Of all the Clongowes Jesuits mentioned in *A Portrait*, Bro. Hanly is the only one actually buried in 'the little graveyard of the community' (265). Bro. Michael lighting the infirmary fire is mentioned in *Ulysses*, p. 781.

152. See, e.g., the picture of the late Bro. Eugene Duffy in *The Clongownian*, Christmas 1897, p. 6.
153. *The Rhetorician*, 28 April 1888.
154. In Stephen's dream, Bro. Michael the newsbringer and Parnell the newsmaker become confused.
155. On Parnell, see Lyons.
156. *Students' Ledger*.
157. *Students' Register*.
158. Ellmann, p. 32.
159. *Students' Ledger*.
160. Kenny–Devitt correspondence, 18 October 1891 (Clongowes Archives). Fr Kenny did not write the year on his letters, but it can usually be deduced from the content.
161. Ibid.
162. Lyons, p. 486.
163. Ibid., p. 531.
164. Kenny–Conmee correspondence (Clongowes Archives). 'Crisis' was evidently the current word for the situation, on one side at least. The Bishop of Ossory, Dr Brownrigg, referred to 'this terrible crisis' in a letter to Archbishop Walsh two days earlier (quoted in Lyons, p. 543). The Belvedere *Ledger* contains the following entry for the 24 December 1890: 'Various newspapers during the crisis. Xmas. £1–0–0.'
165. *Students' Ledger*.
166. See *The Clongownian*, 1932, p. 61.
167. Lidderdale and Nicholson, pp. 118, 122, 127. Hackett wrote to Miss Weaver that he had been at Clongowes with Joyce: 'I can bear testimony to the reality of his description' (p. 122). According to the authors, Joyce was unable to recall that they had been at school together. This was not surprising since Hackett did not come till September 1893 (*Students' Ledger*).
168. He receives a glowing obituary in *The Clongownian*, 1955, pp. 25–27. Francis Hackett, poet and historian, and Florence Hackett, playwright, were members of this family.
169. His grave is first on the left as you enter the graveyard. The Littles lived at 6, New Brighton, Monkstown, Co. Dublin. Stan Little was one of four brothers in Clongowes (*Students' Register*).
170. George A. Little, pp. 213–18.
171. Ibid., p. 217: 'So great was the nervous reaction that great efforts had to be made to relieve the all-pervading melancholy among the boys. On the funeral day a Prefect had even to sit up for the night in the Third Line dormitory to lessen the emotional fears of the small boys.'
172. *Prefect's Journal*, 1889 and 1890; *Minister's Journal*, 1889. Death would also have been one of the considerations at the annual retreat, but in Clongowes Joyce was always too young to attend this.
173. *A Portrait*, pp. 343, 361. Little's was not the only death in Clongowes in Joyce's time. On 29 March 1890, Bro. Peter Temple, the sacristan, died, aged seventy-two. This death would not, of course, have had any similar impact on the boys, who attended neither the Requiem Mass nor the Funeral (*Minister's Journal*).

174. See p. 51 above.
175. Conversation with Fr B. Lawler, S.J. (Clongowes 1921–26) in Clongowes, 25 August 1981.
176. *Prefect's Journal*, 1 March 1890. The further extract below is from the entry for Tuesday 4 March.
176a. The term 'smugging' occurs in *Ulysses* where the narrator of the 'Cyclops' episode recalls a night with two shawls 'up in a shebeen in Bride Street after closing time . . . hugging and smugging. . . .' (407).
177. It is true, however, that the records on which such a judgment is based are somewhat incomplete.
178. *Punishment Book.*
179. *Students' Register.*
180. *Prefect's Journal*, 1884–85.
181. Ellmann, p. 27.
182. *Informations of the Novices.*
183. Finegan, p. 52.
184. 28 April 1888.
185. See p. 16 above; Joyce was at the celebration for these results.
186. April 1891 and 29 November 1890.
187. Curiously, this description fits Fr Daly in old age considerably better than it does the man Joyce would have known, as can be seen by comparing the two extant photographs. The first was taken in 1888, the second in 1914 when Fr Daly was sixty-seven. But there is no evidence to show that Joyce ever saw him again after he left Clongowes.
188. *The Clongownian*, 1930, pp. 78–79. The 'lightly cropped' hair would explain Fleming's nickname 'Baldyhead'.
189. *Province News*, 1930, p. 66.
190. *The Clongownian*, 1930, p. 78.
191. *The Rhetorician*, 14 December 1889.
192. See *The Clongownian*, 1960, p. 6.
193. Anderson, ed., p. 499.
194. 'He had sometimes watched the faces of prefects as they "pandied" boys with a broad leather bat . . .' (*Stephen Hero*, p. 214). A large number of different line and gallery prefects would have been responsible for administering physical punishment during Joyce's time. These would have included Mr William Gleeson, from 1889 onwards. He was a gallery prefect in 1889, assistant to the Higher Line Prefect (Fr Fegan, doubling as Minister) in 1890 and Lower Line Prefect in 1891. He is one of only three Jesuits who retains his own name in this chapter. This may be, as Sullivan (pp. 38–39) suggests, because of his reputation as a cricketer. Later in life his energy and devotion to all forms of sport was a legend among Jesuits: 'Even at the age of fifty, when he was a seasoned missioner, those who lived with him at the Crescent relate that, when at home between missions, he would walk out to Mungret, play a soccer match with the College boys, walk back to Limerick, play a hockey match with the Crescent team and after it all would appear that evening at recreation as the most sprightly of the community!' (*Province News*, 1951, p. 80).

Mr Gleeson in *A Portrait* serves a symbolic purpose, so that his character acquires a certain ambiguity. As Sullivan (p. 35) remarks, 'There was nothing ambiguous about the real-life Mr Gleeson.'

195. The Fr Dolan incident in *A Portrait* is echoed twice in *Ulysses* – in the 'Aeolus' episode (171) and in the 'Circe' episode (667) where Fr Dolan actually 'appears'. For all his apparent solemnity in the classroom, Fr Dolan is able to laugh about the incident later with the rector (*A Portrait*, p. 320).

196. 1863–67. See O'Mahony in Ryan, ed., pp. 150–51.

197. This is clear in letters from Fr General to Fr Provincial and from the latter to Fr Conmee.

198. There is an affectionate, unsigned tribute by Fr Henry Fegan in *The Clongownian*, 1910, pp. 305–07.

199. *The Clongownian*, 1933, p. 93.

200. Con Little, eldest brother of Stanislaus, writing in *The Clongownian*, 1931, p. 32.

201. Ibid.

202. Ibid.

203. Ibid.

204. According to Fr Cyril Power, in a conversation in Clongowes on 27 July 1976. Fr Power was received into the Society of Jesus by Fr Conmee whom he recalled as 'very pleasant, a great man, a real gentleman'.

205. *The Clongownian*, 1960, p. 7.

206. H. Fegan, *The Clongownian*, 1910, p. 306.

207. C. Little, *The Clongownian*, 1931, p. 32.

208. Fr Conmee is mentioned sixty-seven times in *Ulysses*. On three occasions he is called 'Don John Conmee' (286–87, 667), Joyce's 'bland and courtly humanist' (see Ellmann, p. 28). His chivalry makes him seem to belong 'in times of yore' (286). In the 'Circe' episode, when Fr Dolan's image is evoked, 'Don John Conmee' appears, 'mild, benign, rectorial, reproving', and says: 'Now Fr Dolan! Now. I'm sure that Stephen is a very good little boy' (667). This extrapolates from a report Mr Dedalus gives his wife in *A Portrait* of a conversation between Fr Dolan and Fr Conmee. There is a hint of betrayal in Fr Conmee's making a joke of Stephen's heroic protest, over dinner with Fr Dolan and the rest of the community (319–20). But in *Ulysses*, Stephen thinks of himself as 'a child Conmee saved from pandies' (242). Bloom remembers him as 'distinguished looking' (98). In the 'Wandering Rocks' episode, he is pictured as walking in the fields of Clongowes, hearing 'the cries of the boys' lines at their play, young cries in the quiet evening. He was their rector: his reign was mild' (287).

209. The bicycle house was just beyond the infirmary – Stephen must have been on his way out to the playground when he was knocked down.

210. See p. 28 above.

211. Sullivan, p. 233.

212. *Students' Ledger*, f. 132.

213. The Prospectus states: 'Before removing a pupil from the College

during the school period, three months' notice will be required; but a fortnight's notice will be sufficient whenever a boy is withdrawn at the Summer vacation; and it is strongly recommended that, as far as possible, boys be removed only at that period. Boys who are not to remain in College beyond the Winter half, should be withdrawn during the Christmas vacation' (Sullivan, p. 233).

214. This offers the only valid comparison for the procedure in 1891. In 1888 only an informal list of the boys in each class was made out. In 1890, no list of any kind was kept.
215. Ellmann, p. 761, n. 57.
216. Ibid., p. 34.
217. Ibid., on this name for the Joyce's house at 23 Carysfort Avenue.
218. Information about how the account was made out and what individual items in the account referred to is based on a blank form contained in Guard Book A. Details from Joyce's account come from the entry in the *Students' Ledger*, f. 132.
219. See Ellmann, p. 34.
220. The later efforts to do so date from 1901. The Bursar of the time, or someone on his behalf, went through the *Ledger* and attempted to tie up the many loose ends to be found there. He would have known nothing about the circumstances of Joyce's departure.
221. Gorman, p. 39.
222. Fr Kenny to Fr Devitt, 21 September 1891. For date, see note 160 above. As provincial, all the Clongowes books would have been available to Fr Kenny's inspection.
223. Fr Kenny to Fr Devitt, 23 October 1891.
224. M. F. E(gan), *The Clongownian*, 1931, p. 32. John Horgan remembers him as 'rather remote in the Castle . . . dignified, aloof, the final Court of Appeal' (*The Clongownian*, 1955, p. 13).
225. Sullivan, p. 51. Sullivan speaks of Joyce's 'three and a half years' at Clongowes' (p. 14) but does not give any decisive evidence for his assertion that he left 'some time before Christmas, 1891' (p. 51). Stanislaus Joyce said his brother left 'after four years or so' (*My Brother's Keeper*, p. 61).
226. *My Brother's Keeper*, p. 60.
227. Ibid. These visits, on which parents and family were entertained (see p. 82), would have been what suggested to Simon Dedalus that the Jesuits 'lived well': 'You saw their table at Clongowes. Fed up, by God, like gamecocks' (*A Portrait*, p. 319).
228. Quoted by John Horgan in *The Clongownian*, 1955, p. 11. O'Connor's recollection presupposes that Joyce was still in Clongowes in the winter term of 1891 and that he stayed long enough for O'Connor to notice him.
229. Hans Walter Gabler, 'The seven lost years of *A Portrait of the Artist as a Young Man*', in Staley and Benstock, pp. 35–36.

Chapter 2: Belvedere College 1893–98 (pp. 84–142)

1. Ellmann, p. 34.
2. Ibid.
3. Ibid., p. 35.
4. *My Brother's Keeper*, p. 70.
5. As stated by Sullivan, p. 67, Ellmann, p. 35, Scholes & Kain, p. 112, and Anderson ed., p. 504.
6. Fr Conmee's health was frequently mentioned in letters to him in Clongowes from the provincial Fr T. P. Brown, prior to 1888. The subject recurs in the general's letters to several Irish provincials in the nineties.
7. The general's replies are in the Province Archives.
8. The general, Fr Martin, mentions Homburg, Carlsbad, Aix-les-Bains, Buxton, Harrogate and Lisdoonvarna in his letter of 14 October 1893.
9. *Prefect of Studies' Book*.
10. See the discussion, below, on Belvedere's falling numbers. More pupils meant a reduction of debt. Even if they paid no fees, pupils who won exhibitions or other distinctions helped to finance the school. The Intermediate Board made payments to the schools on the basis of their success in examinations.
11. Both are mentioned in the *Prefect of Studies' Book*, where the class-lists were kept in 1900–01. In that year Charles began in 2nd Junior Class but was 'sent down' in October to 2nd Preparatory (1st division). George was in 1st Preparatory, a year behind him. He died on 9 March 1902. (Ellmann, pp. 97–98). By 1900–01, Stanislaus was in Middle Grade.
12. *Cash Book,* 7 September 1894.
13. Byrne, p. 21.
14. As can be seen in the *Cash Book*. Miss Fleming, then about fifty, and Joyce met in the house in Eccles St and did not like each other. Joyce made her 'Mrs Fleming', who cooks and darns socks for the Blooms at the same address, in *Ulysses* (Byrne, p. 88).
15. See William Magennis, 'A disciple's sketch of Father T. A. Finlay', *The Belvederian*, 1931, pp. 19–23; George O'Brien, 'Father Thomas A. Finlay, S.J. 1848–1940', *Studies,* 29 (1940), pp. 27–40.
16. *The Belvederian*, 1940, pp. 29–30.
17. T. A. F(inlay), 'The old Belvedere and the new', *The Belvederian*, 1930, pp. 4–5.
18. See Fr William Delany's letter to Mr Callan MP, quoted in Morrissey, p. 390.
19. Finlay, *art. cit.* See also *The Belvederian*, 1906, p. 19. No. 5 Great Denmark St had already been rented for some years prior to its purchase.
20. R. Campbell S.J., 'Belvedere College seventy years ago,' *The Belvederian*, 1937, p. 9.
21. Campbell, *loc. cit.*
22. *The Belvederian*, 1906, p. 19. R. M. Kain, 'Epiphanies of Dublin', in Staley and Benstock, p. 105 thinks he finds a description of Belvedere in

Fr Conmee's meditations in *Ulysses,* p. 287. But the Belvedere drawing-room is not 'ceiled with full fruit clusters'.

23. *The Belvederian*, 1906, p. 19.
24. Byrne, p. 15.
25. Ibid., p. 146
26. To speak of 'the yard' in this context is ambiguous. In Joyce's time 'the yard' in Belvedere meant the same as 'the square' in Clongowes, a latrine just behind the Finlay Building, entered at the foot of the present stairs. Boland was supposed to have written a graffito 'on the slates in the yard' (330). Hence Ennis had 'gone to the yard' (357). The garden known to Joyce and his contemporaries is now gone, to be replaced by a concrete yard. It is to 'the yard' in this sense that my own text refers.
27. William Dawson, *The Belvederian*, 1910, p. 181 also speaks of the Middle Grade classroom as 'number two', with reference to the same period.
28. p. 85.
29. Fr Cullen published a small devotional periodical, *The Irish Messenger of the Sacred Heart*, still extremely popular, from this office.
30. See Finlay, *art. cit.*, p. 4; *The Belvederian*, 1932, p. 11.
31. p. 69.
32. McKenna, p. 192.
33. See letter of Fr General to the provincial, 12 April 1894.
34. Finlay, *art. cit.*; *The Belvederian*, 1930, p. 4.
35. *Prefect of Studies' Book*. Eugene Sheehy's memory that the number 'did not . . . exceed 120' (Sheehy, p. 1) is slightly exaggerated.
36. Province Archives.
37. *The Belvederian*, 1931, p. 19; Sheehy p. 1.
38. *The Belvederian*, 1940, p. 64.
39. Ibid., 1908, p. 147.
40. Ibid., 1953, p. 10.
41. The timetable in Belvedere is based on the list of 'Religious Exercises in College' current in 1888 and probably unaltered in Joyce's time except for the date of the annual retreat; the 'Science School' Ledger mentioned below, containing times of classes; William Dawson, 'Mr Dempsey – an appreciation', *The Belvederian*, 1910, p. 181; and indications in *A Portrait*. Thus the two afternoon classes, mathematics and religious knowledge, are indicated in chapter 3 (357).
42. See Sheehy, p. 5. This was also one of the times when boys were sent to be pandied, like Leo Dillon in 'An Encounter' (*Dubliners*, p. 32).
43. There was also benediction on First Fridays.
44. See *Stephen Hero*, pp. 27–28. Wheeler was succeeded as bursar and vice-president of UCD in 1901 by Fr Joseph Wrafter, producer of 'Aladdin' in Clongowes while Joyce was there.
45. *Prefect of Studies' Book*, f. 65. The archaic 'Third of Grammar', still in use in Clongowes, does not appear in this book, which refers only to 'Third Grammar'.
46. *Cash Book*. On the lot of lay-teachers in this period, see Sexton, unpublished thesis.
47. *My Brother's Keeper*, pp. 70–71.

48. See also *Ulysses*, p. 611.
49. *Informations of the Novices.*
50. Also mentioned in *Ulysses*, p. 49.
51. See Ellmann, ed., p. 108, where Joyce complains of having been taught by Fr Maher.
52. See Ellmann, p. 20.
53. Based on other entries in the *Prefect of Studies' Book*.
54. Benstock and Benstock, p. 112 mistakenly puts Lawless in Clongowes.
55. Sheehy has a story about him, pp. 2–3.
56. Lenehan features in another of Sheehy's stories, pp. 5–6, about Fr Henry's wager. 'Frenchie' MacDonald and Paget O'Brien Butler are mentioned, pp. 10–11.
57. *Ulysses*, pp. 134–41. He reappears in pp. 597–98.
58. See Benstock and Benstock, p. 121.
59. It is anachronistic to represent them still at Belvedere in 1904. Both entered Rudiments in April 1894 and Eugene, the younger, left in 1899, a year after his brother (Sheehy, p. 1). See also *A Page of Irish History*, p. 613. By 1895 their address in the *Cash Book* is Eccles St. They must have moved later to Belvedere Place.
60. See *Ulysses*, p. 209.
61. Apart from the similarity of the names, Joseph Wilkins did later become a priest and Mr Wilkins did go to 8 o'clock Mass every day in Gardiner St. (*The Belvederian*, 1928, p. 194).
62. Byrne, p. 146.
63. Cosgrave lived at 5 Synnott Place.
64. Byrne, p. 27; *A Page of Irish History*, pp. 608–09.
65. Another of Joyce's friends later on, Oliver Gogarty, of 5 Rutland Square East, was in Elements in 1890–91.
66. Ellmann, p. 762, n. 77. The Connollys lived at 6 Russell Place.
67. Ellmann, *loc. cit.*
68. Wallis is 'a stranger' to Stephen (323). The suggestion in Anderson, ed. that Wallis is 'perhaps Vincent Connolly' (p. 505) cannot be correct.
69. James Joseph Shuley has two addresses in the *Prefect of Studies' Book*: 7–8 Capel St and 206 Clonliffe Road.
70. On 13 November 1894 Mr Nash paid fees 'for boys'.
71. Obituary by Eugene Sheehy in *The Belvederian*, 1913, pp. 153–54. Justin Tallon's address in 1893 was 31 Gardiner Place.
72. As is clear from the preceding paragraphs, the statement of Anderson, ed. that Fallon is 'the only Belvedere student identified by name' (p. 518) is mistaken.
73. e.g. Sutton, Kinsealy, Castleknock (on the north side); Blackrock, Kingstown (on the south).
74. Other boys lived at 9 Windsor Avenue and 8 Glengariff Parade, two of the Joyces' later and less fashionable addresses. One boy's father was in prison.
75. Joyce referred to 'our friendly companionship in boyhood and youth' in a letter of condolence when Eugene Sheehy's father died in 1932 (Sheehy, p. 9).

76. Lady Maxwell, whom Fr Conmee passes so respectfully at the corner of Dignam's Court (*Ulysses*, p. 282), also had sons – Arthur and William – in Belvedere in Joyce's time. The Maxwells lived in North Great George's St.

77. See Lyons *passim* on Sullivan and Clancy.

78. The *Cash Book* records payments from Mr John C. Clancy of St Fintan's Cottage, Sutton and North Richmond St, for his son Charles Boyce Clancy. A ledger for 1890–91 records a payment in October from Mr John Clancy, sub-sheriff. See Ellmann, pp. 43–44.

79. Gorman, p. 43.

80. *My Brother's Keeper*, p. 71.

81. Ellmann, pp. 37–38. The sale was in early February 1894.

82. Ibid. See also Byrne, p. 147.

83. *The Belvederian*, 1932, p. 11.

84. Ibid., 1910. According to the Reports of Temporary Inspectors (1901–02) Part 1 (Intermediate Education Board for Ireland), Mr Dempsey's 'other qualifications' (i.e. in addition to his 'number of years' experience as a teacher') were: 'Honours, 2nd stage, Mathematics, Kensington' (p. 242). Mr Dempsey taught mathematics as well as English, at least in his later years.

85. See Sullivan, pp. 237–40.

86. *The Belvederian*, 1924, p. 78.

87. Byrne, p. 147.

88. Sheehy, p. 3.

89. *The Belvederian*, 1910, p. 181.

90. Byrne, p. 146.

91. He discontinued wearing glasses on the doctor's advice at some time in 1894 and did not resume them for ten years (Gorman, p. 43).

92. Sheehy, p. 4.

93. Byrne, p. 147.

94. *A Portrait* pp. 327–31; *My Brother's Keeper*, pp. 73–74. Stanislaus says the Joyces were living in Millbourne Lane, Drumcondra, when this incident took place.

95. Reports of Inspectors, 1909–10, Vol. 1, p. 7. The inspector was Mr T. Rea, who visited Belvedere with Messrs R. C. B. Kerin and J. O'Neill on 9 September 1909.

96. *The Belvederian*, 1924, p. 80.

97. Ibid., 1925, p. 177.

98. Ibid., p. 178.

99. See *My Brother's Keeper*, p. 145 for another story about Dempsey, in which the same mildly anticlerical note is struck.

100. *The Belvederian*, 1925, p. 178; Sheehy, p. 4.

101. *My Brother's Keeper*, p. 76.

102. Byrne, p. 147. See *Stephen Hero*, pp. 211–12: 'His people are Westmeath . . . He seems to take a great interest in you . . . He is a very well-read man, Stephen.'

103. Gorman, p. 42; *My Brother's Keeper*, p. 76.

104. Sullivan, pp. 237–38 contains the Intermediate syllabus in English for

1894, including the numbers in Lyster. Other poets on the course were Milton, Gray, Cowper, Goldsmith, Wordsworth, Scott, Southey, Campbell, Moore, Wolfe, Longfellow, Browning, Kingsley and Ferguson.

105. Byrne, p. 23.
106. Finegan, p. 72.
107. *The Clongownian*, 1955, p. 13.
108. Gorman Papers (communicated by Prof. Ellmann).
109. Obituary in *The Belvederian*, 1936, p. 134.
110. McCluskey certainly taught Joyce in this year or the next, if not both. He left in 1895 and the 'Trieste Notebook' contains the following entry: 'McCluskey. When not quite sober he used to set us sums about the papering of a trench and told us we should get cent in the exam' (Scholes & Kain, p. 103).
111. A ledger for the Belvedere 'Science School' is in the Belvedere Archives, covering the years 1893–94. Information about the South Kensington examination held in the college is based on this.
112. 'Secondary education' by S. V. Ó Súilleabháin, C.F.C. in *The Church Since Emancipation: 6 – Catholic Education* (A History of Irish Catholicism, V, Dublin: Gill & Macmillan 1971), p. 63. Background on the link with South Kensington is taken from this essay.
113. All neighbours: Laurence J. Dennehy, solicitor, 32 Mountjoy Square; John Healy, professor of languages, 17 Temple St; John V. Duggan, civil servant, 163 Clonliffe Road.
114. Ellmann, p. 40.
115. All information on the Intermediate examinations is taken from Intermediate Education Board for Ireland, *Examination Papers* 1899.
116. Results: see pp. 110–11; Sullivan, p. 237.
117. Ellmann, pp. 41–43.
118. Ibid.
119. The sum of £33 mentioned in *A Portrait* suggests that the incident belongs to 1897, the only year when Joyce won precisely this amount (Anderson, ed., p. 509).
120. Ellmann, pp. 40–41.
121. Gorman Papers (see n. 108). Sullivan's problem about too many language teachers (pp. 91–92) is illusory: Loup, Ryan and McErlean were never on the staff at the same time.
122. *Informations of the Novices*.
123. Joyce called Henry 'a fanatical convert who wore whiskers' (Gorman Papers). No other source mentions Fr Henry's 'whiskers'.
124. O'Mahony, *art. cit.*, p. 153.
125. *Province News*, June 1928, p. 75.
126. Ibid.
127. Gorman Papers.
128. Kenner, p. 123.
129. He taught Stanislaus Greek: *My Brother's Keeper*, p. 73.
130. Ellmann, p. 47.
131. Scholes & Kain, p. 99.

132. Byrne, pp. 146–47.
133. *My Brother's Keeper*, p. 79.
134. Ellmann, p. 57. The identity can be recognised by comparing Fr Butler with Sheehy's picture of Fr Henry, p. 8.
135. *Dubliners*, p. 31.
136. For information, see Intermediate Examination Board, *Examination Papers 1895*.
137. Results: see p. 116–17; Sullivan, p. 237.
138. *My Brother's Keeper*, pp. 82–83.
139. *A Page of Irish History*, pp. 608–09
140. *The Belvederian*, 1907, p. 58. He later entered the Indian civil service.
141. Sullivan, p. 116.
142. McKenna, p. 99.
143. 'Fr Arnall' appeals to 'the prefects and officers of the sodality of Our Blessed Lady and of the sodality of the Holy Angels to set a good example to their fellowstudents' (363). Fr Tunney is presumably the 'Fr Tierney' Ellmann refers to (p. 58).
144. 'Notes to *Stephen Hero*', p. 18 (Scholes & Kain, p. 68).
145. *The Belvederian*, 1907, pp. 113–15. The report is not signed, but Fr McDonnell, the sodality director in that year, as well as a member of the staff in the 'Messenger Office', would be the appropriate and most likely person to have written it.
146. *The Belvederian*, 1940, p. 65.
147. Sullivan, p. 100.
148. *The Belvederian*, 1935, p. 11.
149. Ellmann, p. 48, quoting Stanislaus, places Joyce's early sexual encounters 'during his fourteenth year' and probably in the twelve months following his reception into the sodality.
150. Montgomery St, Tyrone St and Mabbot St – all later renamed.
151. *My Brother's Keeper*, pp. 84–87.
152. Sullivan, p. 116.
153. Ellmann, p. 52 attributes Joyce's leading role rather to his scholarship than to his sodality position.
154. *A Page of Irish History*, p. 613.
155. *The Belvederian*, 1909, p. 89.
156. Despite the difficulties of dating the retreat, referred to by Scholes & Kain, pp. 112ff., Ellmann is surely right in placing it after Joyce's first sexual experiences and before his final year in school (p. 49).
157. Sullivan, pp. 131–32.
158. See Sullivan, pp. 130–31. Fr Arnall seems to patronise his audience and then seeks to frighten them into virtue, inspiring in Stephen a feeling of regression to childhood – as both innocent and vulnerable. The images of Clongowes which the sight of 'his old master, so strangely rearisen' (361) evokes all come from the first, pre-Christmas episode in Clongowes, rather than the second, when Stephen was pandied.
159. Thus Fr Conmee gave the Clongowes retreat in September 1893, when he had been transferred from Belvedere to UCD and no longer had classroom obligations (*Prefect's Journal*). The Clongowes retreat-

director in 1896 was Fr Bernard Vaughan, Joyce's 'Fr Purdon' in *Dubliners*, who appears under his own name in *Ulysses*, p. 281.

160. See chapter one.
161. Sullivan, p. 128.
162. Ellmann, p. 49.
163. *The Belvederian*, 1929, p. 277. Canon R. O'Kennedy wrote of seeing Fr Cullen about 1889 in Gardiner St (where he also worked while in Belvedere) 'bent in his characteristic attitude of humility and thought, his cap pushed down on his head and his Roman cloak about him' (*The Clongownian*, 1922, p. 247).
164. Sullivan, p. 129 mistakenly refers to Fr Cullen as having had the office of spiritual father added to his other tasks in 1897.
165. *Prefect's Journal*.
166. McKenna, p. 295.
167. Ibid.
168. Ibid., p. 122.
169. Ibid., p. 198.
170. A scrapbook of notices and circulars from Fr Tomkin's rectorship (1900–08) contains a printed card with the retreat timetable.
171. McKenna, p. 295.
172. '. . . he walked home with silent companions' (*A Portrait*, p. 364).
173. *A Portrait*, pp. 361–64; 364–68; 371–79; 382–93.
174. Thrane, pp. 172–98.
175. Ibid., p. 197.
176. McKenna, vii–viii.
177. The Belvedere copy has no date. But this date is given in the Milltown Park catalogue. According to the same source, vol. 1 originally appeared by itself in 1831. Gobinet explains that he only later recognised the need for fuller treatment of the sacraments of Penance and the Holy Eucharist (p. 276).
178. pp. 276–493.
179. The effects of sin, pp. 312–33; hell, pp. 318–26.
180. p. 318.
181. McKenna, p. 401.
182. Ibid., pp. 152–53. 'On the margins of his sermon-books there are numerous pencil-marks, capital letters and other figures – evidently part of some system of mnemonics which he used in committing his discourses to memory' (p. 34). On this basis, Fr Cullen clearly used Gobinet for preaching.
183. Ibid., p. 20.
184. 'The occasion of undertaking it was, my being called to the direction of youth' (v).
185. Ibid., p. 318.
186. Ibid., p. 319.
187. Ibid.
188. Ibid., pp. 319–26.
189. Sullivan (pp. 138–41) discusses the bearing of Fr Cullen's Sodality Manual on Joyce's sermons.

190. Also omitted by Joyce in Fr Arnall's retreat, although the topic is treated in the edition of Pinamonti Joyce would have known (Thrane, *art. cit.*, pp. 173–74). From Joyce's outline of the sermons in his 'Notes for *Stephen Hero*' he included one on heaven for the 'morning after 4th Day' (Scholes & Kain, p. 69).

191. McKenna, pp. 34, 97.

192. MS. in the hand of the late Fr Rupert Coyle, S.J., who left Belvedere in 1913.

193. It is probably by virtue of his position as prefect of the sodality that Stephen 'sat in the front bench of the chapel' listening to Fr Arnall (361).

194. *Prefect's Journal.*

195. Ellmann, p. 50.

196. *My Brother's Keeper*, p. 97.

197. Conversation with the late Fr Cyril Power in Clongowes, 20 July 1976. Fr Power remembered Jeffcoat in Tullabeg in 1908, the last year of his life. He was always 'very delicate' and is a rather implausible candidate for the role in which Stanislaus casts him, even supposing he had been a priest at the time.

198. *My Brother's Keeper*, p. 95.

199. Results: pp. 130–31; Sullivan, p. 237.

200. Intermediate Education Board for Ireland, *Examination Papers 1897*.

201. In the 'Trieste Notebook', under the heading 'Jesuits', Joyce wrote: 'I learnt Latin prosody from the rhymes of Fr Alvarez' (Scholes & Kain, p. 102). On Alvarez, see Benstock & Benstock, p. 47.

202. The Italian papers for 1897 and 1898 are not available to me.

203. Ellmann, pp. 36–37.

204. Ibid., p. 54.

205. He persevered with natural philosophy and his mark improved – from 100 in 1895 to 175 in 1897. The maximum was 500 in each case.

206. *The Belvederian*, 1910, p. 182. The list also includes two medals for history and geography (also Dempsey's subject) awarded to A. C. J. Cox.

207. Stoer's name occurs in *Ulysses* and Morkan's in both *Ulysses* and *Dubliners*: see Benstock & Benstock, pp. 156, 129.

208. Sullivan, p. 117. The date was 17 December.

209. Ellmann, p. 50.

210. Sheehy, p. 8.

211. A member of the Clongowes community in 1888–89, but Joyce is unlikely to have had any contact with him. He is favourably mentioned as rector in *My Brother's Keeper*, p. 143.

212. On the gymnasium, see *The Belvederian*, 1908, p. 148.

213. Intermediate Education Board for Ireland, *Reports of Temporary Inspectors* (1901–02) Part 1 (Dublin), p. 243.

214. *My Brother's Keeper*, p. 88.

215. Gorman Papers.

216. Ibid.

217. Ellmann, pp. 55–56.

218. *Province News*, June 1928, p. 76.
219. Stanislaus Joyce, quoted in Anderson, ed., p. 516.
220. Fʀ Henry began theology in Louvain in 1888 but came back to Dublin the following year. The reference to 'jupes' (414) presumably derives from the rector's year in Belgium.
221. Simon Dedalus mimics the hotel-keeper (270) and Fr Conmee (320).
222. See *The Belvederian*, 1960, pp. 58–59.
223. This must be the date of the play: there were no gymnastics before 1898. The *Cash Book* has this entry; 'June 2nd. Elvery & Co. for Theatre Gymnastics £12–2–4'. The date in Anderson, ed. (p. 505) cannot be correct.
224. *Vice Versa: or a lesson to fathers* (London 1882; revised 1883; with additions 1894) by Thomas Anstey Guthrie ('F. Anstey').
225. Ellmann, p. 57. Bloom took part in this play, in one of the girls' parts, in High School (*Ulysses*, pp. 648–49).
226. *Vice Versa: Made from F. Anstey's Story*, by Edward Rose (French's acting edition, London; n.d.). References to the play are from this edition.
227. Sheehy, pp. 8–10; *My Brother's Keeper*, p. 102.
228. Ellmann, p. 57. Sullivan, p. 91 is mistaken in thinking that Mr McErlean was not in Belvedere in that year. See *My Brother's Keeper*, p. 103.
229. Schouppe was based on the Malines Catechism.
230. Schouppe, vi.
231. Results: p. 140–41; Sullivan, p. 237.
232. Intermediate Education Board for Ireland, *Examination Papers 1898*.
233. Gorman, pp. 45–46. See Sullivan's discussion, pp. 75–77.
234. See n.202 above. Joyce also took commercial French, in which he got 102 out of 200. His mathematics and natural philosophy marks were derisory.
235. Ellmann, p. 57.
236. Byrne, p. 157.

# Bibliography

## UNPUBLISHED MATERIAL

**Manuscripts**

*Clongowes Wood College Archives*
Guard Book A
    Scrapbook 'containing, in no particular order or sequence, scraps and gobbets of information about the past of the college: school notices, newspaper items, announcements, programs of plays, debates, athletic events, and so on' (Sullivan, p. 241). The Prospectus of 1886, the blank account sheet and the programme of 'Aladdin, or The Wonderful Scamp' are contained in this book
Letters of Provincials to Rectors of Clongowes, 1885–92
*Minister's Journals,* 1889, 1890
*Prefect's Journal,* 1881–1905
*Prefect of Studies' Custom Book*
*Punishment Book,* 1881–97
    Begun at Tullabeg (with 'St Stanislaus' College Tullamore' printed on the cover) and continued in Clongowes after the amalgamation in 1886
*The Rhetorician,* 1888–92
    Five issues produced in Clongowes, 1888–90, and four produced in Dublin, 1890–92 by the Rhetoric class of 1888
Rules of the boys of Clongoweswood
*Students' Ledger* H 1886–1907
*Students' Register,* 1886–94

*Belvedere College Archives*
*Cash Book,* 1861–97
Fr Rupert Coyle MS
Ledger, 1890–91
*Prefect of Studies' Book,* 1889–93; 1900–01
'Science School' Ledger, 1892–94
Scrapbook
    Much more modest than the Clongowes Guard Book, containing some printed notices from the rectorship of Fr Tomkin (1900–08)

*Irish Province Archives*
*Informations of the Novices,* 1860–95
    Brief autobiographies written on admission
Letters of Generals to Irish Provincials, 1885–98
Fr Henry Lynch MS
*Menology of the Irish Province of the Society of Jesus*

*Croessmann Collection (Southern Illinois University Library)*
Gorman Papers (excerpt communicated by Prof. Richard Ellmann, 8 July 1981)

## Typescripts

Morrissey, T., S.J., 'Some Jesuit contributions to Irish education: with special reference to 16th and 19th centuries' (unpublished thesis submitted to University College, Cork; 1975)

Sexton, P. F., S.J., 'The lay teachers' struggle for status in Catholic secondary schools in Ireland between 1878 and 1937' (unpublished thesis submitted to the University of Birmingham; 1972)

PUBLISHED MATERIAL

## Books

Anderson, Chester G., *James Joyce and his world*, London: Thames and Hudson 1967

Anderson, Chester G., ed., James Joyce, *A Portrait of the Artist as a Young Man*. Text, criticism and notes: New York: The Viking Press 1968

Benstock, Shari and Benstock, Bernard, *Who's He When He's At Home: A James Joyce Directory*, Urbana: University of Illinois Press 1980

Byrne, J. F., *Silent Years: An Autobiography with Memoirs of James Joyce and Our Ireland*, New York: Farrar, Strauss and Young 1953

Corcoran, T., S.J., *The Clongowes Record 1814 to 1932*. Dublin: Browne and Nolan Ltd n.d.

Corish, Patrick, ed., *A History of Irish Catholicism* V, Dublin: Gill and Macmillan 1971

Ellmann, Richard, *James Joyce*, New York: Oxford University Press 1959

Ellmann, Richard, ed., *The Letters of James Joyce*, II, London: Faber and Faber 1966

Fathers of the Society of Jesus, *A Page of Irish History: Story of University College, Dublin 1883–1909*, Dublin & Cork: The Talbot Press Ltd 1930

Finegan, Francis, S.J., *Limerick Jesuit Centenary Record 1859–1959*. Limerick: Sacred Heart College 1959

Gobinet, Charles, *Instructions for Youth in Christian Piety Taken from the Sacred Scriptures, and the Writings of the Holy Fathers*, translated from the French, a new edition, Dublin: James Duffy & Sons n.d.

Gorman, Herbert, *James Joyce: A definitive biography*, London: John Lane – The Bodley Head 1941

Guthrie, Thomas Anstey ('F. Anstey'), *Vice versa: or a lesson to fathers*, revised edition, London 1883

Hodgart, Matthew, *James Joyce: A Student's Guide*, London: Routledge & Kegan Paul 1978

Hutchins, Patricia, *James Joyce's World*. London: Methuen 1957

Intermediate Education Board for Ireland, *Examination Papers 1894–98*, Dublin: Browne & Nolan 1894–98

Intermediate Education Board for Ireland, *Reports of Temporary Inspectors 1901–02*, Part 1, Dublin

Intermediate Education Board for Ireland, *Reports of Inspectors 1909–10*, Vol. 1, Dublin

Intermediate Education Board for Ireland, *Results of Examinations 1894–98*, Dublin: Browne & Nolan 1894–98

Joyce, Stanislaus, *My Brother's Keeper*, London: Faber & Faber 1958

Kenner, Hugh, *Dublin's Joyce*, London: Chatto & Windus 1955

Lewis, Samuel, *A Topographical Dictionary of Ireland*, London: S. Lewis & Co. 1837

Lidderdale, Jane and Nicholson, Mary, *Dear Miss Weaver: Harriet Shaw Weaver 1876–1961*, London: Faber and Faber 1970.

Lunn, Arnold, *The Harrovians*, London: Methuen 1913

Lyons, F. S. L., *Charles Stewart Parnell*, London: Collins 1977

McKenna, Lambert, S.J., *Life and Work of Rev. James Aloysius Cullen, S.J.*, London: Longmans, Green & Co. 1924

Noon, William T., S.J., *Joyce and Aquinas: A Study of Religious Elements in the Writing of James Joyce*, New Haven: Yale University Press 1957

*Parliamentary Gazeteer of Ireland, The*, Dublin: A. Fullerton & Co. 1846

Power, William, S.J., *The King's Bell and Other Verses*, Braine-le-Comte (Belgium): Zech and Son 1910

Rose, Edward, *Vice Versa, Made from F. Anstey's Story*, London: Samuel French Ltd n.d.

Ryan, John, ed., *A Bash in the Tunnel: James Joyce by the Irish*, Brighton: Clifton Books 1970

Scholes, Robert and Kain, Richard M., eds., *The Workshop of Dedalus: James Joyce and the Raw Materials for A Portrait of the Artist as a Young Man*, Evanston, Illinois: Northwestern University Press 1965

Schouppe, F. X., S.J., *Abridged Course of Religious Instruction, Apologetic, Dogmatic, and Moral: for the Use of Catholic Colleges and Schools*, new edition, thoroughly revised, London: Burns and Oates 1880

Schwickerath, R., S.J., *Jesuit Education: Its History and Principles Viewed in the Light of Modern Educational Problems*, St Louis, Mo.: B. Herder 1904

Sheehy, Eugene, *May It Please the Court*, Dublin: C. J. Fallon Ltd 1951

Staley, Thomas and Benstock, Bernard, eds., *Approaches to Joyce's Portrait: Ten Essays*, University of Pittsburgh Press 1976

Sullivan, Kevin, *Joyce Among the Jesuits*, New York: Columbia University Press 1958

Tindall, William York, *The Joyce Country*, New York: Schocken Books 1972

**Periodicals**

*The Belvederian*, 1906– . Published annually.

*Catalogus Provinciae Hiberniae Societatis Jesu*, 1860–1930. Dublin: Browne & Nolan. Printed for private circulation only

*The Clongownian*, 1895– . Published bi-annually, 1895–1900, annually thereafter

Little, George A., 'James Joyce and Little's Death', *The Irish Rosary* 16 (1962), pp. 213–18

O'Brien, George, 'Father Thomas A. Finlay, S.J., 1848–1940', *Studies* 29 (1940), pp. 27–40

*Province News (Ireland and Australia)* (later *Irish Province News*), 1925–
  Printed for private circulation only
Thrane, J. R., 'Joyce's Sermon on Hell: its Source and its Backgrounds',
  *Modern Philology* 57 (1960), pp. 172–98

# Index

174

179